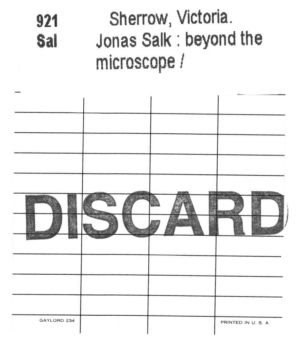

Jonas
Salk

REVISED EDITION

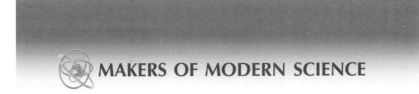

MAKERS OF MODERN SCIENCE

Jonas Salk

Beyond the Microscope

REVISED EDITION

~~EVERGREEN LIBRARY~~

VICTORIA SHERROW

CHELSEA HOUSE
PUBLISHERS

An imprint of Infobase Publishing

*To my sister, Marianne Jones, whose love of learning
and unwavering support inspire me every day*

Jonas Salk: Beyond the Microscope, Revised Edition

Chelsea House
An imprint of Infobase Publishing
132 West 31st Street
New York NY 10001

ISBN-10: 0-8160-6180-7
ISBN-13: 978-0-8160-6180-8

Library of Congress Cataloging-in-Publication Data

Sherrow, Victoria.
    Jonas Salk: beyond the microscope / Victoria Sherrow.—Rev. ed.
        p. cm.—(Makers of modern science)
    Includes bibliographical references and index.
    ISBN 0-8160-6180-7
    1. Salk, Jonas, 1914—Health—Juvenile literature. 2. Virologists—United States—
Biography—Juvenile literature. 3. Poliomyelitis vaccine—Juvenile literature. I. Title.
QR31.S25S54 2008
579.2092—dc22   2006033429

Chelsea House books are available at special discounts when purchased in bulk
quantities for businesses, associations, institutions, or sales promotions. Please call
our Special Sales Department in New York at (212) 967-8800 or (800) 322-8755.

You can find Chelsea House on the World Wide Web at
http://www.chelseahouse.com

Text design by Kerry Casey
Cover design by Salvatore Luongo
Illustrations by Elisa Scherer and Chris Scherer

Printed in the United States of America
MP FOF 10 9 8 7 6 5 4 3 2 1
This book is printed on acid-free paper.

CONTENTS

PREFACE

S cience is, above all, a great human adventure. It is the process of exploring what Albert Einstein called the "magnificent structure" of nature using observation, experience, and logic. Science comprises the best methods known to humankind for finding reliable answers about the unknown. With these tools, scientists probe the great mysteries of the universe—from black holes and star nurseries to deep-sea hydrothermal vents (and extremophile organisms that survive high temperatures to live in them); from far away galaxies to subatomic particles such as quarks and antiquarks; from signs of life on other worlds to microorganisms such as bacteria and viruses here on Earth; from how a vaccine works to protect a child from disease to the DNA, genes, and enzymes that control traits and processes from the color of a boy's hair to how he metabolizes sugar.

Some people think that science is rigid and static, a dusty, musty set of facts and statistics to memorize for a test and then forget. Some think of science as anti-human—devoid of poetry, art, and a sense of mystery. Yet science is based on a sense of wonder and it is all about exploring the mysteries of life and our planet and the vastness of the universe. Science offers methods for testing and reasoning that help keep us honest with ourselves. As physicist Richard Feynman once said, science is above all a way to keep from fooling yourself—or letting nature (or others) fool you. Nothing could be more growth-oriented or more human. Science evolves continually. New bits of knowledge and fresh discoveries endlessly shed new light and offer new perspectives. As a result, science is constantly undergoing revolutions—ever refocusing what scientists have explored before into fresh, new understanding. Scientists like to say science is self-correcting. That is, science is fallible and scientists can be wrong. It is easy to fool yourself and it is easy to be fooled by others, but because new facts are constantly flowing in, scientists are continually refining their work to account for as many facts as possible. So science can make mistakes but it also auto-corrects.

Each volume of the Makers of Modern Science set presents the life and life work of a prominent scientist whose outstanding contributions in his or her field have garnered the respect and recognition of other prominent colleagues. These profiled men and women were all great scientists, but they differed in many ways. Their approaches to the use of science were different: Niels Bohr was a theoretical physicist whose strengths lay in patterns, ideas, and conceptualization, while Wernher von Braun was a hands-on scientist/engineer who led the team that built the giant rocket used by Apollo astronauts to reach the Moon. Some had genius sparked by solitary contemplation: geneticist Barbara McClintock worked alone in fields of maize and sometimes spoke to no one all day long. Others worked as members of large, coordinated teams. Oceanographer Robert Ballard organized ocean-going ship crews on submersible expeditions to the ocean floor; biologist Jonas Salk established the Salk Institute to help scientists in different fields collaborate more freely and study the human body through the interrelationships of their differing knowledge and approaches. Their personal styles also differed: biologist Rita Levi-Montalcini enjoyed wearing chic dresses and makeup; McClintock was sunburned and wore baggy denim jeans and an oversized shirt; nuclear physicist Richard Feynman was a practical joker and an energetic bongo drummer.

The volumes in the Makers of Modern Science set offer a factual look at the lives and exciting contributions of the profiled scientists—in the hope that readers will see science as a uniquely human quest to understand the universe and that some readers may be inspired as well to follow in the footsteps of these great scientists.

ACKNOWLEDGMENTS

I would like to thank Frank K. Darmstadt, executive editor, who provided valuable guidance and editing suggestions during the preparation of this new edition.

I am also grateful to the following people and institutions for their help in providing images for the book:

Kenneth R. Harris, Sr., Director, Roosevelt Warm Springs Development Fund, and Mike Shadix, Archivist, Roosevelt Warm Springs Institute for Rehabilitation, Warm Springs, Georgia; John D. Harvith, Senior Associate Vice Chancellor, University News and Magazines; University of Pittsburgh, Pittsburgh, Pennsylvania; Karen L. Jania, Head, Access and Reference Services, Bentley Historical Library, University of Michigan, Ann Arbor, Michigan; Gina Kirchweger, Science Writer; The Salk Institute for Biological Studies, La Jolla, California; and, Sheila R. Spalding, Archivist; Children's Hospital, Boston Boston, Massachusetts

INTRODUCTION

As the 21st century began, people looked back at events that had defined the previous hundred years. The 20th century saw huge advances in science and technology, including wireless communication and digital computers. The power of atomic energy was harnessed, and humans walked on the Moon. Surgeons transplanted human hearts and other vital organs. Geneticists worked to unravel the secrets of heredity and DNA.

The media reexamined these events, highlighting people who had played key roles in 20th-century life. One of the recurring names was that of Dr. Jonas Salk, a medical researcher and founder of the Salk Institute for Biological Studies. Salk developed the first effective vaccine to fight a crippling viral disease called poliomyelitis, known as "polio," which had become epidemic during the 1900s.

People hated polio not just for the suffering it caused but because it usually struck babies and children. Some victims died, while others were left paralyzed. A few were never again able to breathe on their own. The disease also seemed to strike at random, attacking people from all walks of life, in clean homes and dirty ones, on farms and in cities. No place seemed safe from the "summer monster."

Although polio no longer poses a threat in the United States or most other nations, millions of Americans still recall the terror that polio once brought into their lives. They can also remember hearing the good news on April 12, 1955: A field test showed that a new vaccine could prevent polio. Around the nation, bells chimed, car horns honked, and fire sirens blared. Reporters declared that people were rejoicing as if a war had ended. And, in a sense, the polio vaccine did end a war, one that was waged against an unseen and devastating enemy. The vaccine brought down a disease that held the power to steal lives.

The leader of the research team that developed that vaccine was Jonas Salk, and people regarded him as a hero. Salk went on to study other diseases, including cancer and AIDS, and he sought ways to improve public health. He founded a unique scientific institute where leading scientists can collaborate and conduct research useful in diagnosing, preventing, and treating diseases. Inspired by his vision of a better world, Salk also worked for various humanitarian endeavors.

The revised edition of this book describes Jonas Salk's medical research and his lifelong efforts to promote scientific and human progress on a global scale. The son of immigrants, he grew up in a working-class family and succeeded through talent and hard work. His story shows how scientists build upon the achievements of others while bringing their own perspective to the challenges they face in the laboratory and in the field. Often, as Salk liked to say, scientific progress is a matter of asking the right questions and then being open to possibilities. In the case of polio, people around the nation also aided medical research in ways that have never occurred before or since.

The revised edition brings readers up to date regarding Salk's final years and the current work of the Salk Institute. It also describes the global campaign to eradicate polio from the planet, since the fight against this disease has continued in developing nations. Salk worked with other scientists to develop more effective vaccines and delivery systems that protect more people from polio and other diseases. During his lifetime, Salk was part of an ongoing scientific debate over the merits of killed-virus vaccines versus live-virus vaccines. He continued to defend the principle behind killed vaccines even after his own vaccine was replaced by Albert Sabin's live but weakened vaccine, which is taken by mouth not injection. This story also did not end with Salk's death, as the Centers for Disease Control (CDC) changed its policy during the late 1990s, when it recommended that physicians resume using inactivated polio vaccine (IPV).

In 2005, 10 years after Salk's death, special events marked the 50th anniversary of the long-awaited announcement that the world had a vaccine against polio. The disease was close to being extinguished as people gathered to remember Salk's medical triumph and to honor the man and his far-reaching legacy.

1

Early Years in New York

Jonas Salk once said that he grew up during a crucial period of history, one that also ushered in a "golden era" for science. Significant historical and political events influenced his youth, and advances in science paved the way for his own work. Two pivotal events occurred very early during his childhood: World War I began in 1914, the year Salk was born, and a devastating epidemic struck his hometown of New York City when he was not quite two years old, living in East Harlem with his parents.

That summer of 1916 began much as usual, with young people throughout New York anticipating good times with friends and family at playgrounds, theaters, amusement parks, swimming pools, and the seashore. Outside New York, World War I still raged in Europe. Many Americans were discussing whether the United States would join its allies, Britain and France, in the fight against Germany, especially after a German U-boat sank the passenger ship *Lusitania* in 1915, killing 128 Americans. Patriotism was running high, and officials in New York were planning special festivities for the upcoming Fourth of July.

These plans were suddenly replaced by fears over survival itself as an epidemic hit New York and several other states. Epidemics—sudden, large-scale outbreaks of disease—sweep across cities, regions, and nations, even continents, leaving death or damaged health in their wake. Smallpox, bubonic plague, and typhus have caused some of the worst epidemics in history. This time it was polio, a disabling disease that had been confounding scientists for centuries.

A Dreaded Disease

Beginning in the 1900s, polio became a serious public health problem in the United States and other industrialized nations with high standards of living. Scientists could not explain why. They did know, however, that this disease had existed since ancient times. Skeletons dating back to 3700 B.C.E. had deformed arms and legs, much as polio did. An Egyptian carving from around 1580–1350 B.C.E. shows a man with a withered leg, typical of a polio attack. The Greek physician Hippocrates (460–377 B.C.E.) described a disease that caused paralysis in some patients. Medical accounts of individual cases and small outbreaks appeared in the 1800s and epidemics began to occur in the 1890s.

As the epidemic of 1916 spread, New Yorkers dreaded the sights and sounds that meant polio had struck again: An ambulance racing down the street with bells clanging . . . a quarantine sign nailed to a building in their neighborhood . . . lists of victims' names in the newspaper . . . the word EPIDEMIC! printed in thick black letters.

Children in New York also felt the fear. They saw the newspaper headlines and quarantine signs. They saw people being rushed to the hospital. Some saw polio survivors on the streets, struggling to walk with heavy metal braces or crutches. Says author Jane S. Smith, "Living through a polio epidemic was like living in a city in a bomber's path. Each night you wondered if you'd wake up the next morning; each morning you checked to see if any of the neighbors had been hit."

This slab shows an ancient Egyptian with a shriveled leg typical of a polio attack. (Photo Researchers)

By 1916 doctors had been studying polio for more than a century. The first published clinical description came from Michael Underwood, a British pediatrician. In his 1789 medical textbook,

Treatise on the Diseases of Children, Underwood described a "palsy" that "sometimes seizes the upper, and sometimes the lower, extremities; in some instances, it takes away the entire use of the limbs it has attacked, and in others, only weakens them."

As physicians in various countries treated patients with this disease, they gathered more information. In Italy, surgeon Giovanni Battista Monteggia (1762–1815) saw several children whose illness began with a fever and progressed to paralysis. Monteggia wrote that within days after they became ill, the children's "extremities [were] quite paralyzed, immobile, flabby, hanging down, and no movement is made when the sole of the foot is tickled." Like other doctors, he noted that most victims were under age two.

German physician Jakob von Heine (1800–79) studied patients during an outbreak in 1836. He observed fever, congestion, irritability, convulsions, and pain before paralysis occurred, usually in the legs. Heine concluded that the disease attacked motor nerves in the spinal cord, which control muscle movements, but he saw no signs of brain damage. Heine correctly deduced that this was a separate disease, not a form of palsy. In a paper he presented in 1840, he discussed treatments, including baths, exercises, bracing, and simple surgical procedures.

Until the mid-1800s, autopsies—physical exams of people who have died—showed no visible damage in the brain or spinal cord of polio victims. When stronger microscopes became available, researchers could see damage in the spinal cord. French scientist Jean-Martin Charcot (1825–93) studied sections of spinal cord taken from people who had developed paralysis. He found a loss of nerve cells in the anterior horn of the gray matter in the cord. Since the gray marrow in the spinal cord was affected, doctors began calling the disease poliomyelitis. This comes from the Greek words *polio,* meaning "gray," *myelos,* referring to damaged areas in the spinal cord, and *itis,* meaning "inflammation."

As information accumulated, more articles about polio appeared in professional journals and medical books. The five-volume text, *System of Medicine by American Authors,* included a scholarly chapter on polio called "Infantile Spinal Paralysis." It was written by Mary Putnam Jacobi (1842–1906), who held two degrees in medicine and one in pharmacy. As a student in Paris, Mary Putnam had studied neuropathology and visited Charcot's clinic. She then practiced medicine in New York City, where she married Abraham Jacobi, a prominent pediatrician. Physicians practicing in the United States often referred to this text when treating polio patients.

In 1890, Swedish pediatrician Karl Oscar Medin presented a detailed paper about polio at an international conference in Germany. Acknowledging the contributions of Medin and Jakob Heine, some doctors used the name "Heine-Medin disease." Others called it infantile paralysis because most victims were very young children. One of Medin's students, Dr. Ivar Wickman, conducted door-to-door interviews in 1905, when an epidemic hit Sweden. Wickman concluded that most people were infected at a local school. He also theorized that many people contracted mild cases that did not cause major symptoms because polio never reached their nervous system. This theory would later be proved correct.

Doctors still wondered what sort of organism caused polio and whether or not it was contagious. One answer came in 1908, when Austrian-American Dr. Karl Landsteiner (1868–1943) isolated a

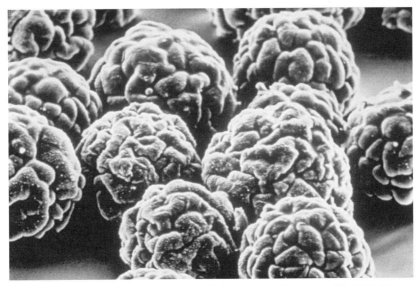

Polioviruses, as seen under one of today's high-powered microscopes (World Health Organization)

specific virus that causes polio. Three years later, Dr. Simon Flexner (1863–1946) showed that poliovirus could be transferred in monkeys. His laboratory team managed to capture and study a nondeadly form of poliovirus. Flexner also realized that polio is contagious.

While research continued, new polio outbreaks occurred, primarily in Scandinavian countries, France, and the United States. Cases were also reported in Asia. In 1844, Swedish doctors documented 44 cases. The first actual epidemics striking at least 100 people occurred in Norway (1868), Sweden (1881), and Vermont (1894). Worse outbreaks occurred after 1900. Sweden documented 1,031 cases in 1905—the largest epidemic to that date. New York City recorded between 750 and 1,200 cases in 1907. The state was hit again in 1911, along with Iowa and Ohio. The following summer, Buffalo, New York, was hit. Scientists noted that most epidemics were occurring in the United States, Scandinavia, Canada, the British Isles, Australia, and Switzerland, but they could not explain why. They wondered if this was a new version of polio, or even a different disease. Modern methods of sanitation and better health care had curbed many illnesses, but polio was growing more common.

Once a person was diagnosed, doctors could offer no cure. Treatments were limited and sometimes harmful. During the 1800s many doctors followed the standard practice of applying ice to the spine and rubbing mercury ointment on the skin along the spine. This could cause blisters that required additional treatment. Doctors also tried in vain to revive paralyzed limbs with electrical stimulation. As late as the 1920s, some doctors advocated vigorous massage during the acute phase of polio, a practice that was later shown to aggravate the condition.

Desperate Measures

Faced with a serious epidemic in 1916, New York City health officials tried to prevent polio from spreading by closing camps, theaters, public pools, Sunday schools, and other places. Public health workers removed patients from their homes or set up quarantines in homes where families seemed able to follow strict instructions. On June 30, 1916, the front page of the *New York Times* carried instructions from the health department:

Keep children out of the streets as much as possible and be sure to keep them out of the houses on which the Department of Health has put a [quarantine] sign. . . . This is the disease which babies and young children get; many of them die, and many who do not become paralyzed for life. Do not let your children go to parties, picnics, or outings.

Parents warned their children: Stay away from crowds. Do not go to the playground. Do not go swimming. Do not drink from a water fountain. Do not go to the theater.

New Yorkers kept their homes extra clean and told their children to wash frequently. They shut their windows, despite the heat. Parents tied small cloth bags with a lump of strong-smelling camphor around their children's necks. This chemical, used to kill moths, was supposed to repel polio. Some people sprayed special liquids into their noses to kill germs. As rumors spread, animals began taking the blame. People rounded up stray cats and dogs and killed hundreds every day. On July 26, 1916, a headline in the *New York Times* announced "72,000 Cats Killed in Paralysis Fear."

The health commissioner expressed the frustration of battling polio: "In epidemics of typhoid fever and most other diseases the health authorities know exactly what to do. But fighting infantile paralysis consists largely in doing everything that seems effective in the hope that some of the measures taken will be effective."

Fear drove thousands of people to flee the city for rural areas, the mountains, islands, and even other countries. Wealthy people sent their children away in private trains. Roads leading out of New York were jammed with cars, and long lines formed at bus and railroad stations. In order to leave, people had to show a doctor's certificate stating that nobody in their household had polio. Towns and resorts outside New York used roadblocks to keep out people who might be infected. Armed sheriffs patrolled the roads and ordered cars with children under age 16 to return to the city.

When polio season ended that fall, statistics showed that in New York 9,000 people had caught polio and 2,448 died. Twenty states reported 7,179 deaths and 27,000 people left paralyzed. Only 20 states required doctors to report polio cases to the government in 1916, so the actual numbers must have been higher. It was the largest polio epidemic thus far, with worse to come. Like other New

"A Piercing Pain . . ."

Charlene Pugleasa was 13 years old when she came down with polio in September 1953 in her hometown of Sudan, Minnesota. In *A Paralyzing Fear: The Triumph Over Polio in America*, she

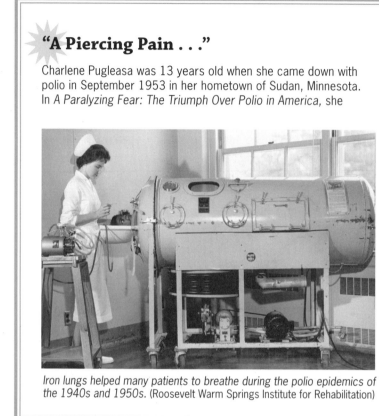

Iron lungs helped many patients to breathe during the polio epidemics of the 1940s and 1950s. (Roosevelt Warm Springs Institute for Rehabilitation)

Yorkers, Dora and Daniel Salk felt that fear in 1916, followed by relief when the epidemic ended. For the moment at least, their son Jonas was safe.

A Gifted Student

Jonas Salk was born on October 28, 1914, in a tenement flat apartment located in the East Harlem section of New York City. He was the firstborn of Dora (Dolly) Press Salk and Daniel Salk, both of whom were Russian Jewish immigrants. At age 16, Dora Salk had found work in a garment factory where she soon rose to the position of supervisor. Daniel Salk, a designer of ladies' describes what happened that Friday night when she went to the movies with her friends: "I only remember being real sick in the movie. My back ached, my body hurt, and . . . it was a piercing pain, a bad headache, a sore throat." During the two-mile walk back home, Charlene was unusually tired and her legs felt weak. Within two days, she had developed a high fever and was drifting in and out of consciousness. Pain shot through her limbs, and her muscles went into spasms. A doctor who came to her home on Monday told her parents, "I'm afraid Charlene has infantile paralysis."

That night, she was rushed to a hospital and put into an isolation room. Despite her pleas, the hospital would not let her mother stay. For more than a month, she remained in the hospital for treatments and physical therapy. During that time, she saw other patients arrive, including babies, toddlers, and a pregnant woman who delivered her baby from inside an *iron lung*. When Charlene finally went home, her mother took over her treatments and helped her do her exercises each day. She also completed her schoolwork at home until she returned to classes at the end of December but says "I never could take phys. ed. I felt unusual because of that." Although she had endured fear, loneliness, and a painful rehabilitation, Charlene Pugleasa felt very grateful that she was once again able to walk after her polio attack.

blouses and neckwear, worked at the same factory. They fell in love and were married. Although life was sometimes difficult, the Salks lived with great optimism. They appreciated the economic opportunities and political and religious freedom they found in America. They worked hard to learn English and support their family, which grew to include Herman, born in 1919, and Lee, born in 1926.

Dora was known as an efficient homemaker and ambitious mother who set high standards for her sons. Salk later said, "She wanted to be sure that we all were going to advance in the world." All three became professionals with doctoral degrees—Herman as a veterinarian and Lee a clinical psychologist.

By the time Jonas started school, the Salks had moved to the Bronx section of New York. Young Jonas enjoyed the usual childhood activities but often chose to spend time alone thinking or reading. He later said, "I tended to observe and reflect and wonder." Slender, with dark hair and eyes, Jonas wore glasses for nearsightedness. A former teacher recalled that he "read everything he could lay his hands on." People noticed his strong reasoning abilities and curiosity. He asked probing questions and expressed his opinions, though in a polite way.

At age 12 he was accepted into a special tuition-free high school for gifted male students. Townsend Harris Hall was operated by City College of New York. Students completed their coursework in just three years instead of the usual four. About 200 students were chosen each year from among thousands of applicants. Fellow students later recalled that Salk did not stand out. One classmate called him a "nice, but unremarkable boy."

Scientists often choose their future careers at a young age, but Jonas Salk took only one science course—physics—in high school. He later explained, "As a child I was not interested in science. I was merely interested in things human, the human side of nature." He enjoyed history, philosophy, and literature, including poetry and works by Ralph Waldo Emerson, Henry David Thoreau, and Roger Bacon. He also read biographies of people he admired, including Abraham Lincoln and Louis Pasteur. Salk had no definite career plans but was seriously considering law. He did intend to do something important with his life.

In 1930 Salk graduated near the top of his high school class. Like many teenagers, he felt that childhood was ending, but his real life had not begun. He later recalled, "I knew I was competent. I knew I had proved it by achieving that which I was supposed to achieve, time and time again. The remainder of childhood was for me a period of patient waiting, and not much else." Childhood was now over, and Salk prepared for the challenges of college and career.

Scientist in
the Making

Just as Salk's early years were marked by major historical events, so were his college years. These experiences were helping to forge what Salk's biographer Richard Carter called the "man-oriented or humanistic outlook" that Salk would bring to his scientific work and research institute. As an adult, he said, "I remember seeing our troops coming back on Armistice Day [when World War I ended] in 1918. I recall even as a young child being perplexed by seeing wounded soldiers in the parade. Then I became aware of anti-Semitism [prejudice against Jews] in the world and the difficulties that occurred during the Depression."

Instead of feeling overwhelmed by such problems, Salk thought that he could make a difference. Growing up, he had observed how hard work and determination enabled his parents to build a better life. His own intelligence, diligence, and sense of purpose had brought him academic success and the chance for a college education. The next decade would see Salk moving from prelaw into science and on to medical school, where he would begin to pursue his life's work.

Change of Career

At age 15 Salk entered City College of New York as a prelaw student. He was interested in social problems and politics, two topics that were much discussed during the Great Depression, which had begun the previous October. The stock market crashed that month, and investors lost millions of dollars. During the next five years, thousands of businesses closed and banks failed. About one-fourth of U.S. workers lost their jobs. Millions of men, women, and children became homeless, and hungry people lined up to eat at free soup kitchens run by charities and local governments.

Despite the Depression, Salk managed to continue his education. His career plans changed, however, when he became captivated by what he called "the magic of nature." Salk later said that "curiosity" had led him to enroll in a chemistry class during freshman year. Once there, he became excited about science. Here was a place where he could use both logic and creativity to examine old ideas and find solutions to important problems. Salk switched his major to chemistry and decided to attend medical school. He would become a medical researcher—one who studies diseases and finds ways to prevent, treat, and cure them.

In 1934 Salk received a bachelor of science degree in chemistry. During the admissions interview for New York University Medical School, he was asked why he wanted to become a doctor. Salk said he was interested in medical research. When the interviewer pointed out that researchers did not earn much money, Salk replied, "There is more in life than money." That fall he started medical school, with the aid of scholarships and $1,000 that his parents had managed to save. Salk earned money working as a laboratory technician during the school year and camp counselor in the summer.

Like other future doctors, Salk studied anatomy, physiology, microbiology, bacteriology, pathology (disease processes), and pharmacology. He spent many hours in the laboratory. At City College he had not earned outstanding grades or joined clubs or other activities. In medical school, however, Salk excelled academically, in the lab, and in patient care.

He especially wanted to understand how the body fights infection. Infecting substances—bacteria or viruses—contain chemical material that scientists call *antigens.* Antigens prompt the body to make substances called antibodies that are sent out to eliminate the problems that bacteria or viruses can cause. Antibodies help the body to destroy unwanted microorganisms and prevent them from

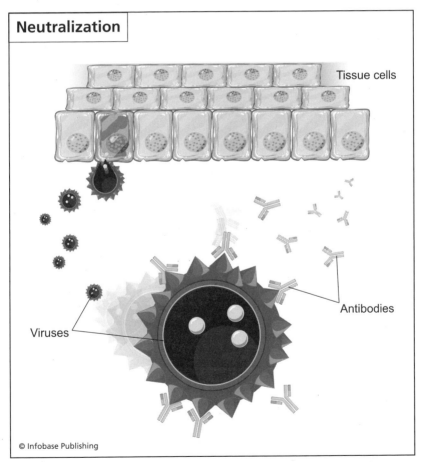

Neutralization

Tissue cells

Antibodies

Viruses

© Infobase Publishing

Antibodies work by binding to certain sites on viruses so that these viruses cannot bind with other cells in the body.

spreading, reproducing, and releasing toxins—poisonous substances—that damage healthy cells. These antibodies then can fight off a future attack by the same bacteria or virus, providing immunity.

To polish his laboratory skills, Salk left school in 1935 to accept a fellowship doing advanced work with biochemist Dr. R. Keith Cannan, his chemistry professor. A respected researcher, Cannan had noticed Salk's abilities and keen interest in research. Salk later said that he seized the opportunity when Cannan had called him into his office to invite him to spend a year in his lab. One of Salk's assignments was to find a more efficient way to concentrate bacteria so they could be separated from the broth cultures in which they were grown. Through experimentation, Salk was able to freeze the cultures so that bacteria clumped together. This led to the 1938 publication of his first professional paper, which described the technique.

After returning to medical school in 1936, Salk was attending a lecture on bacteriology and immunology when he had an insight that deeply influenced his thinking. During a 1991 interview conducted for the Academy of Achievement, Salk said that "a light was turned on" as he listened to the professor:

> We were told in one lecture that it was possible to immunize against diphtheria and tetanus by the use of chemically treated toxins, or toxoids. And the following lecture, we were told that for immunization against a virus disease, you have to experience the infection, and that you could not induce immunity with the so-called "killed" or inactivated, chemically treated virus preparation.... What struck me was that somehow both statements couldn't be true. And I asked why this was so, and the answer that was given was in a sense, "because."... It didn't make sense and that question persisted in my mind.

After the lecture, Salk continued to wonder why a vaccine made with killed viruses could not prevent disease while a vaccine made with killed bacteria could do so. This did not make sense to him, but it would be several years before he had the chance to test his ideas while studying influenza and polio viruses.

Polio remained in the news while Salk completed medical school. As more cases surfaced each summer, scientists debated why polio was spreading, especially among adults. They questioned whether modern sanitation and improved cleanliness might actually put more people at risk. Many disease-causing organisms, including polio, were widespread before modern sewage systems and indoor plumbing became available. Polioviruses had been found in human waste products. Scientists theorized that people would become immune if they were exposed to polioviruses early in life. They would gain the natural protection that results when a person fights off an infectious organism and survives. But children born after 1900 were exposed to fewer germs, including polioviruses, than previous generations.

Looking for a Treatment

With no means of preventing or curing polio, people tried various treatment methods. Many physicians followed the approach that Dr. Robert W. Lovett, a physician and author who organized the first polio clinic at Children's Hospital Boston, had advocated since 1916. It required complete rest during the initial stage of the disease, followed by warm water, massage, and exercise.

A new trend emerged during the 1930s, however, when doctors began splinting limbs to keep them motionless. This approach was later abandoned again in favor of moving the affected limbs.

The best-known post-polio treatment came from Elizabeth Kenny, a self-trained nurse who had worked in rural Australia. Kenny wrapped very hot wool bandages around the arms and legs of polio patients. She promoted the use of massage and movement of the afflicted limbs after the initial polio attack. "Sister Kenny," as she was known, said that her methods prevented further stiffening and loss of muscle tone. Her approach was based on her mistaken belief that the muscle problems were caused by spasms rather than damage to the nerves that controlled the muscles. Even so, many people found that her treatment methods were helpful. Others rejected Kenny's ideas. Critics claimed that her treatment helped only people who would not have been permanently paralyzed anyway.

The prognosis for paralyzed patients remained bleak, and some people were doomed to spend the rest of their lives in iron lungs. People longed for a truly effective weapon against the dreaded virus.

It also seemed likely that polio came in different forms, including mild, nonparalytic versions, so doctors probably missed many cases. Polio historian John R. Paul explains that polio in young babies "is mainly a mild, passing infection. They have so-called unapparent infections, produce antibodies [substances that fight infection], and become immune—save for a few who die or the rare infant who survives as a cripple." This meant that people who survived infancy before 1900 would likely have been exposed to polio. They would not get the disease later on, when it usually causes more damage.

In addition, doctors thought that more powerful strains of polio had developed through the years. Viruses can become stronger as they pass from one organism, or person, to another.

Salk's growing interest in viruses led him to seek out Dr. Thomas Francis, a prominent researcher and the head of New York University's Department of Bacteriology. In 1938 he approached Francis in his lab, asking, "Is there anything I can do?" Francis later said that Salk impressed him as "a good young man, interested, with ideas." He invited Salk to spend free periods in his lab, studying viruses.

At that time, virology was a relatively new field, but scientists were making progress. A few years earlier, Francis had been the first American to isolate an influenza virus, and he hoped to develop vaccines against that disease. Influenza can pose serious public health threats. In 1918 a pandemic—worldwide epidemic—killed an estimated 20 million people. Francis was investigating ways to immunize people against influenza, and Salk looked forward to taking part in that work.

The Search for Immunity

People have known about immunity for thousands of years, although they did not understand the process itself. The ancient Chinese noticed that people became immune after one attack of smallpox, a highly contagious disease. By the late 1700s smallpox had killed millions of people around the world.

A preventive technique called *ingrafting* emerged in the Middle East. To carry out this technique, people took scabs of infected material from the sores of those who had mild cases of smallpox.

Then they inoculated others by piercing their skin with a needle and inserting infectious material into the broken skin. About a week later the person would suffer a weak case of smallpox, with some fever and sores but without severe scars or death. In 1718 Lady Mary Wortley Montagu, the wife of the British ambassador to Constantinople, brought the idea of ingrafting to England. The English tried it, but with mixed results. Occasionally someone became seriously ill or died. Handling infectious material also posed the risk of spreading smallpox or causing an epidemic.

Dr. Edward Jenner (1749–1823) found a safer method. While working in Gloucester, England, Jenner noticed that milkmaids in

This engraving shows Edward Jenner vaccinating James Phipps against smallpox.
(Corbis)

rural areas did not get smallpox. Local people would say, "Once you get the cowpox, you cannot take the smallpox." Cows with cowpox developed sores on their udders, the part that milkmaids squeeze while milking. Jenner concluded that cowpox was a mild form of smallpox. As a test, he decided to inoculate someone with cowpox material from an infected milkmaid. He scratched the arm of eight-year-old James Phipps with a knife, then placed infectious material in the scratch. As Jenner expected, James developed a fever and headache. His arm grew red and swollen where it was infected. A pustule formed, then turned into a scab. The scab fell off, leaving a faint mark. James Phipps recovered. Six weeks later Jenner exposed James to infectious material from a smallpox patient. James did not get smallpox. He remained immune when Jenner repeated the test 20 times in later years.

Jenner gathered more cowpox material during an epidemic in 1798. He exposed numerous people by using infectious material taken from each patient in turn. Jenner called his technique vaccination, because the infected material came from cows, and *vacca* means "cow" in Latin.

At that time, scientists did not know what causes diseases, although they had seen microorganisms. In 1675 Dutch scientist Antoni van Leeuwenhoek (1632–1723) used small, simple home-made microscopes to study the tiny moving creatures he called "little beasties." He found them in many substances, including drops of water and bits of tartar from his teeth.

During the 1770s Italian scientist Lazzaro Spallanzani (1729–99) studied minute organisms he found in meat broth. He thought they came from the air and multiplied in the broth. Spallanzani saw that new organisms did not grow if he kept the container tightly sealed.

Eventually, scientists learned that microorganisms can cause disease. French chemist Louis Pasteur (1822–95), known as the "Father of the Germ Theory" of medicine, provided some answers. After the 1820s Pasteur and other scientists could examine microorganisms using the basic compound microscope (one with two lenses). During the 1850s Pasteur studied fermentation—the chemical changes that occur when yeast or other organisms grow in fruit juice, turning it into wine. He realized that fermentation results from organisms that enter the juice, not something that already exists in juice and other foods, as people once thought.

Pasteur developed a heating process to destroy unwanted organisms without hurting the wine's flavor. This process—called pasteurization after its inventor—later was used to protect milk from organisms that cause diseases and hasten spoilage. Pasteur became convinced that organisms too small to be seen by the naked eye cause infections. He called them "germs."

At age 55 Pasteur focused his attention on immunity. He learned how to culture—grow—certain "germs" in his laboratory, including the microorganisms that cause cholera in chickens. During those years this disease was epidemic in Europe. Pasteur realized that small doses of this microorganism (later identified as bacteria) could kill birds. During one test, he used organisms from an older culture that had been sitting in his lab for several weeks. The chickens he injected with this old material did not die. To explore this further, Pasteur injected material from fresh cultures into the same chickens and other chickens. Fresh cholera germs killed some chickens, as before. But the birds that had received the aged cholera culture survived. Apparently they were immune, although they never appeared to be sick.

For two years Pasteur continued culturing cholera germs taken from chicken feces. Repeated tests showed that weakened cholera germs could produce immunity. Chicken farmers adopted Pasteur's methods and saved their flocks.

Pasteur proceeded to change germs into less dangerous forms by aging, heating, cooling, exposure to chemicals, and growing them in the tissues of animals that did not get cholera. A changed live germ of this kind is said to be attenuated, meaning "weakened." Perhaps weakened germs could produce immunity without causing serious illness, thought Pasteur.

He next tackled anthrax, a disease that killed thousands of sheep and cattle each year. German scientist Robert Koch (1843–1910) had identified the rod-shaped anthrax bacillus. He found that it assumes different forms during its life cycle. As a spore, or lifeless seed, it lies on grassy areas, where cows, sheep, and other hoofed animals feed. Inside the animal's body, the spore resumes the form of an infectious bacillus, which will multiply and spread. These parasites (organisms that live off another organism) destroy vital organs, causing death.

Koch was the first person to show that a specific bacillus caused a specific disease. He took anthrax bacilli from infected animals and grew them artificially (outside of living tissue) in his lab. Koch went on to isolate other microorganisms, including the bacilli that cause tuberculosis (TB), a lung disease.

Pasteur used Koch's methods to culture microorganisms. In one experiment, he cultured anthrax bacilli, then killed them with phenol, a chemical. He injected this material into sheep, hoping that dead anthrax would produce immunity, as weakened cholera germs did. When he injected those same sheep with live germs, they did not get sick, although live germs did kill sheep that Pasteur had not injected with the killed germs. Pasteur's anthrax vaccine, which

Shown here performing an experiment, Louis Pasteur developed vaccines for cholera, anthrax, and rabies. (Corbis)

saved sheep and cattle throughout Europe, was the first widely used killed-bacteria vaccine.

Pasteur moved on to rabies, called hydrophobia in humans. Rabies was rare but terrifying. A bite from a rabid animal led to seizures, paralysis, insanity, and then death. Pasteur cultured rabies germs from the saliva of infected dogs. To weaken the germs, he dried the saliva on glass slides. When he injected this dried material into healthy dogs, they did not get sick. Pasteur concluded that the rabies germs were either gone or dead. He decided to make a vaccine by growing dried rabies germs in rabbit brain tissue, since rabies targets the brain.

Growing and attenuating—weakening—rabies was difficult. Pasteur placed the germs in one rabbit brain after another. He tried growing rabies in rabbits' spinal cords, and then dried the cords for several weeks. Pasteur learned that rabies has a long incubation period (time lapse between the day of infection and the appearance of disease symptoms). These germs take from four to six weeks to move from the site of a bite to the brain.

Pasteur then inoculated healthy dogs with his dried rabies vaccine. He placed these dogs, along with dogs that had not been vaccinated, inside a pen with a rabid dog. The vaccinated dogs did not get rabies; the others died.

In 1885 a woman begged Pasteur to help her nine-year-old son. Joseph Meister had been bitten 14 times by a dog that seemed rabid. Doctors debated whether Pasteur should use his rabies vaccine. Pasteur himself wondered if it would work before the rabies reached Joseph's brain. And what if the dog did not have rabies after all? Pasteur later said, "I could not sleep the night before the last injection. The material I was using was so deadly, so undiluted, that it killed an unprotected rabbit in less than a day."

Over the next 11 days Pasteur gave Joseph 12 shots. Fortunately he lived and was healthy. Pasteur went on to give hundreds of rabies vaccinations to people who were bitten by rabid dogs. In 1888 he became the director of a new scientific institute that was built in Paris in his honor. Pasteur died in 1895 without ever seeing the minute organism that causes rabies. Today scientists know that it is a virus.

Doctor Salk

During medical school, Salk examined bacteria and viruses under microscopes far more powerful than Pasteur's. He studied the history of vaccinations and learned how they produce immunity against certain diseases. Immunology was a growing field, and through his work with Thomas Francis, Salk was becoming a part of it.

In June 1939 Jonas Salk received his medical degree from New York University. The day after graduation he married Donna Lindsay, whom he had met the previous summer while doing research in the town of Wood's Hole, Massachusetts. The daughter of a dentist, Lindsay grew up in an upper-middle-class family in Manhattan. She earned her psychology degree with high honors at Smith College and began graduate studies at the New York College of Social Work. Donna Salk later said that she appreciated Jonas's idealism and sense of humor. She found him to be a stimulating conversationalist and good dancer.

Before the wedding her father made a special request: Would Salk give himself a middle name? Dr. Lindsay thought that would sound more distinguished. His future son-in-law obliged and became "Jonas Edward Salk."

At age 24 Salk was a full-fledged doctor, with a partner who shared his intellectual interests and desire to improve the world. He had agreed to work in Thomas Francis's lab for a year after medical school before he began his hospital internship. They planned to test different methods of purifying influenza viruses and seek ways to inactivate them so that they could not cause disease while retaining the power to promote immunity. Salk was delighted to be working in an exciting field with one of the nation's foremost researchers. Step by step, he was reaching his goals and gaining the skills and experience he would need to develop life-saving vaccines.

Tracking Down
Viruses

Salk's work in Francis's lab took on a special urgency as World War II began in Europe. Led by Adolf Hitler, Nazi Germany had annexed Austria in 1938 and then invaded Czechoslovakia and Poland in 1939. Poland's allies, England and France, declared war against Germany and its allies, Italy and Japan (together called the Axis), that September.

The war expanded as more countries faced invasion and occupation. Americans again wondered if the United States would join the war, the second global war that Salk had seen during his 25 years. He knew that medical research could help to prevent the kind of epidemic that had killed so many troops during World War I. An influenza vaccine would benefit people in the military and civilians.

The 1940s found Salk completing his medical training and resuming his vital research with Francis to develop such a vaccine and then test it. His work during this decade confirmed his earlier theories about the merits of killed-virus vaccines and brought him recognition as a virologist and epidemiologist.

Busy Years

A two-year internship was a required part of Salk's medical training. He had applied to New York's Mount Sinai Hospital, a large, well-equipped facility with an excellent staff. About 250 outstanding medical school graduates applied each year. Only 12 were selected, and Salk was one of them.

Like his fellow interns, Salk received no salary as he worked long hours and continued to study medicine. He examined and treated patients, attended lectures and meetings, and worked with researchers who hoped to prevent or cure diseases. A colleague later recalled that Salk was "versatile and promising . . . by far the most mature and most reliable. . . . You told him to do something and it got done." Another colleague said that Salk was "a fine clinician and . . . incredibly patient." His fellow interns showed their respect by electing him as president of their group.

Salk showed his leadership skills when he and his fellow interns clashed with the hospital administration. They had decided to wear badges on their jackets to show support for the Allies, but the Mount Sinai administrators told them to stop wearing these political symbols. When Salk stood firm and explained their position, the administrators decided to permit the badges.

During Jonas's internship, Donna Salk worked at the Jewish Child Care Association in New York. The couple sometimes joined other interns and their spouses for the steak dinner that was a Sunday tradition in the Mount Sinai house-staff dining room. Salk also made time for tennis and golf because he believed physical fitness was important.

As his internship came to an end, Salk sought a research position. He and his wife liked living in New York, so he approached some research facilities there. Despite his fine record, he did not receive an offer. Some observers believe that, in at least one case, Salk was rejected because of anti-Semitism (anti-Jewish attitudes).

In October 1941 Salk visited Thomas Francis, who had moved to Ann Arbor to head the newly opened School of Public Health at the University of Michigan. Francis had a grant from the U.S. government to continue studying influenza viruses. Salk decided to join him if he could obtain a National Research Council fellowship to fund his work. Francis wrote a letter on his behalf, saying, "I esteem his abilities highly and would welcome the opportunity to have him work with me."

The grant came through. A few days later, on December 7, 1941, Japanese warplanes attacked the U.S. naval base at Pearl Harbor, Hawaii. The United States Congress declared war on the Axis nations. Salk was informed that he would be called to serve in the medical corps.

The need for influenza vaccines remained urgent, however. During World War I influenza had killed more than 550,000 Americans, 44,000 of them in the military. The Armed Forces Epidemiological Board asked Thomas Francis to develop a vaccine against different strains of influenza, especially Influenza A. Francis

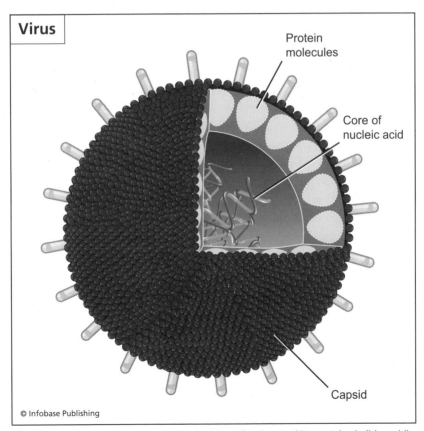

Virus

Protein molecules

Core of nucleic acid

Capsid

© Infobase Publishing

This diagram shows the nucleic acid in the core of a virus and its protein shell (capsid).

wanted Salk to join him, and the board agreed that he could conduct research instead of serving in the corps.

The Salks headed for Michigan, where they rented a small apartment in an old farmhouse, and Donna found a new job as a social worker. Despite the long commute to his lab, Salk liked his rural surroundings and enjoyed planting a vegetable garden. In addition to laboratory research, he taught classes in epidemiology.

At that time influenza, and the body's responses to it, mystified many scientists. Researchers had studied respiratory tissues, seeking clues to immunity. Salk immersed himself in various aspects of influenza research. He was willing to challenge preexisting ideas about how people become immune as he sought to understand how specific viruses interact with the human body and its immune system.

Elusive Enemies

Before 1940 few scientists had been able to study viruses intensively. Viruses are even smaller than bacteria. A million virus particles, placed side by side, equal just one inch. Viruses grow only in specific kinds of living cells, so scientists could not culture them in test tubes or on plates as easily as bacteria and funguses. They could not stain them with laboratory dyes as they did with bacteria in order to identify, measure, and count them.

Scientists began learning about viruses in the late 1800s. In 1886 German scientist Adolf Mayer could not find a bacterial cause for tobacco mosaic disease. Six years later, Russian scientist Dmitri Ivanovski (1864–1920) devised an experiment that showed this disease was caused either by a toxin or some agent smaller than bacteria.

Martinus Beijerinck (1851–1931), a Dutch botanist—a scientist who studies plants—duplicated Ivanovski's experiments during the late 1890s. When Beijerinck pressed the juice from the leaves of the sick tobacco plants, a substance from the juice passed through the porcelain filters he used to strain out bacteria. Although the filter caught the bacteria, this unknown material slipped through. When he rubbed the strained juice on healthy plant leaves, they got tobacco mosaic disease. Beijerinck concluded that an infectious substance caused tobacco mosaic disease. He called it a "contagious living fluid." In 1898 he named the substance "virus," from a Latin word meaning "poison." Beijerinck correctly guessed that viruses grow only in living cells.

Other scientists tried to stain viruses so they could view them under optical microscopes. But viruses resisted staining. They continued to pass through very fine porcelain filters. Scientists had to guess viruses were present by observing whether filtered material still caused disease.

In 1931 Dr. William J. Elford developed a porcelain filter with pores small enough to trap viruses. This showed that viruses were solid particles, not liquid as Beijerinck had thought. That same year Drs. Ernest Goodpasture and Alice Woodruff grew viruses in a sealed hen's egg, called a chick embryo culture. Chick embryos provide an uncontaminated medium for growing microorganisms. (After the early 1940s scientists could use antibiotics to kill bacteria that might affect their test results.)

American biochemist Wendell Meredith Stanley achieved a breakthrough when he crystallized tobacco mosaic virus in 1935. He froze sick plants so that their cells would burst. Then Stanley ground up the leaves and squeezed out juice to obtain a pure form of the virus. He proceeded to check each sample to see if it caused disease in healthy plants. When Stanley had a liquid that satisfied him, he added chemicals that made long crystals form. Dissolved in water, these needle-shaped crystals made healthy plants sick, which showed they were tobacco mosaic virus. Something that appeared dead—crystals—sprang back to life in liquid. Stanley described his experiments in his article "Isolation of a Crystalline Protein Possessing the Properties of Tobacco-Mosaic Virus," which appeared in *Science* magazine that same year. Other scientists expressed skepticism. How could the viruses be alive and yet not alive? Scientists took sides as they tried to classify viruses either one way or the other.

Research conducted during the 1940s would show that viruses are made of nucleic acid, the genetic molecular material found in all living cells as DNA (deoxyribonucleic acid) or RNA (ribonucleic acid). The type of virus is determined by the design of the nucleic acid. About 95 percent of a virus is located in its outer shell, made of protein. The type of protein on the virus determines which kinds of living cells it will invade.

After electron microscopes emerged in 1938, scientists finally could see viruses and their different shapes. Scientists had thought that microorganisms were either bacteria or viruses, but some viruses seemed to fall somewhere in between. An example is the *Rickettsia* that causes typhus; today, scientists classify it as bacteria.

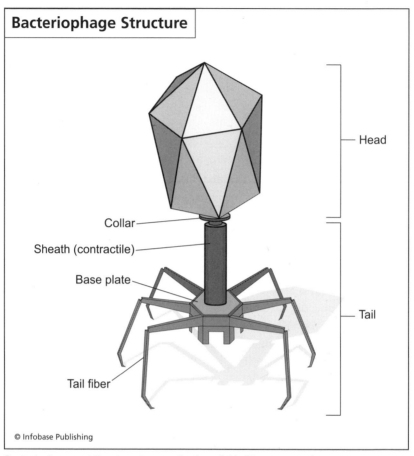

Bacteriophage Structure

Head

Collar

Sheath (contractile)

Base plate

Tail

Tail fiber

© Infobase Publishing

Bacteriophage and the steps in reproduction, divided into two sections over two pages:
- (a) A bacteriophage is a type of virus that attacks bacteria cells.
- (b) During that process, it attaches to the bacteria cell and penetrates it in order to inactivate the cell's own DNA and begin to replicate itself, producing new viruses.

Researchers found major differences between viruses and bacteria. Bacteria can divide into new cells, which continue dividing to make more bacteria. Viruses need a live cell—human, animal, plant, or bacteria—to reproduce. They are intracellular microbes, meaning they enter living cells. They use proteins and other material to live and reproduce. By taking over a cell's life processes, a virus causes damage or death. Cells produce more viruses instead of the proteins or compounds they need to survive. As rapidly multiplying viruses kill cells, they proceed to infect others.

Scientists began to realize that viruses cause many diseases, including rabies, smallpox, measles, and influenza. Polio was also a viral illness. Karl Landsteiner had identified a poliovirus in 1908

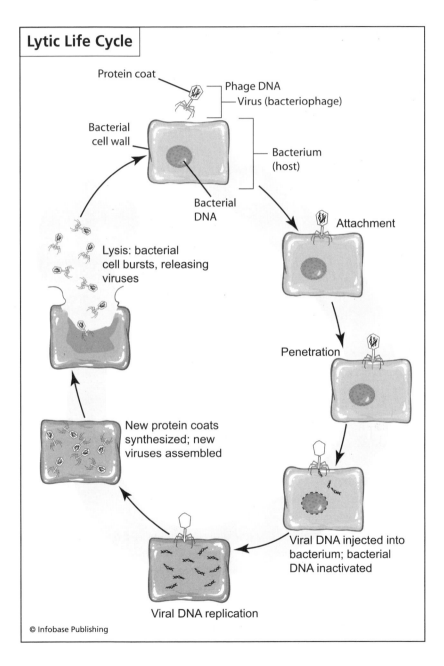

Lytic Life Cycle

Protein coat

Phage DNA

Virus (bacteriophage)

Bacterial cell wall

Bacterium (host)

Bacterial DNA

Attachment

Lysis: bacterial cell bursts, releasing viruses

Penetration

New protein coats synthesized; new viruses assembled

Viral DNA injected into bacterium; bacterial DNA inactivated

Viral DNA replication

© Infobase Publishing

after gathering material from the spinal cord tissue of a child killed by polio. Landsteiner made fluid from the infected tissue and then filtered it. When he injected this material into healthy monkeys, they got sick. This meant that conquering polio would pose the challenges that arise when working with viruses.

Developing an Influenza Vaccine

As Salk worked in the lab at Ann Arbor, he confronted the challenges involved in treating viral illnesses. Antibiotics that kill bacteria do not kill viruses. Viruses use the cell's own material to grow, and the drugs that kill viruses also can kill healthy cells. For that reason scientists have sought ways to prevent viral diseases. Before the 1940s vaccines had been developed against only rabies, smallpox, and *yellow fever*. More antibacterial vaccines were developed, partly because bacteria are easier to grow. Viruses grow in living cells, and maintaining pure live tissue cultures is difficult.

Pasteur and others had still managed to produce antiviral vaccines. They proved that giving people a mild form of a disease, or a disease that closely resembles it, can spark antibody production. This enables the immune system to deactivate the virus if it reappears in the future.

As he and Francis continued their work, Salk carried out various tasks involved with developing a vaccine and evaluating the results. He hoped that blood tests could be used to help evaluate the effectiveness of the influenza vaccine. Salk figured out a way to calculate the amount of antibody in the blood. His tests showed that people with higher levels of antibodies in their blood were more immune to future attacks of disease. This meant that after giving a test vaccine, researchers could test a person's blood to see how much immunity that vaccine had provided.

Their goal was to make a flu vaccine based on a killed virus—one that was no longer able to cause disease. Scientists had long debated the merits of live versus killed vaccines. In a live-virus vaccine, the viruses multiply after entering the body but not enough to cause full-blown disease. This stimulates the defense mechanisms in the blood to make antibodies. Advocates of live vaccines claim that they produce stronger, more lasting immunity because they cause a natural infection—the disease itself, though in a milder, harmless form. The viruses in such a vaccine are called weakened, tamed, or attenuated. On the other hand, vaccines made from killed microorganisms can no longer cause disease, so their supporters claim they are safer. Yet, to be effective, the killed virus needs to keep enough of its original traits to convince the body it faces a real infection.

Salk favored the idea of a vaccine containing more than one strain of flu virus. That way one injection could protect people against different strains. An epidemic of Type A occurred in 1943. Francis's team used this strain in their vaccine to protect people against Weiss Flu, which is a Type A strain. Through preliminary tests, Francis's team found that killed-virus vaccine could stimulate the production of antibody levels as high as those produced by the flu itself. Using the blood test Salk developed, they found a direct relationship between the level of antibodies and the amount of resistance to new attacks of influenza.

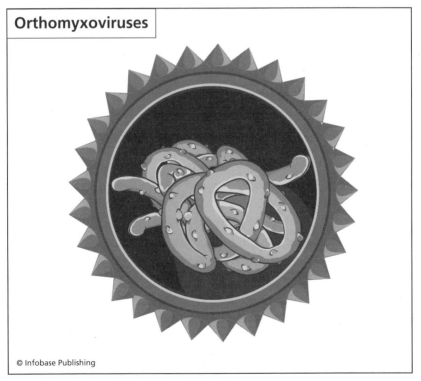

Orthomyxoviruses

© Infobase Publishing

The class of viruses known as Orthomyxovirus includes the influenza virus.

By 1943 Francis had organized field trials to test their influenza vaccine on human volunteers. These were double-blind studies. That meant that some volunteers received real vaccine while others received a placebo (nonmedicinal substance). In a double-blind study, nobody knows who received the real medicinal subject and who received a placebo until the results are gathered and analyzed. This includes the volunteers and the researchers themselves—they are all "blind" until the study is over. This approach aims to prevent bias in analyzing the results.

During the winter of 1943–44, 25,000 people participated in these trials. The results showed that the killed-virus influenza vaccine worked. Newspapers in Ann Arbor and the surrounding area announced that Francis and Salk had developed a successful flu vaccine. Salk was eager to share their findings and gain recognition for his work, so he began writing scientific papers about the influenza research and field test, which he co-authored with Francis and other members of their team. One of these articles, "Experience With Vaccination Against Influenza in the Spring of 1947," was published in the *American Journal of Public Health*. Others articles appeared in the *Journal of Immunology* and the *Journal of Clinical Investigation.*

Salk had been appointed to the United States Army Influenza Commission in 1943, and from 1945 to 1947 he spent many weeks in Europe. Assigned the temporary rank of army major, he conducted studies on influenza and set up laboratories in Germany, where U.S. troops were still stationed. These laboratories were designed to diagnose influenza quickly in order to prevent a postwar epidemic.

Although Salk willingly performed this vital work, he was glad when it ended. He wanted to resume his research and spend more time with his family. At age 33 Salk was regarded as an expert on epidemiology—the science of how and where infectious diseases are spread. He received invitations from the American Medical Association and other scientific and professional organizations to present papers on his work.

After spending nearly six years at the University of Michigan, Salk was eager to run his own lab. He looked forward to applying what he had learned and taking on new challenges. He later explained, "I wanted to do independent work and I wanted to do it my way." As the next chapter will show, he would have that opportunity within a year, thanks to a nationwide effort to defeat polio.

Fighting Polio
in the Lab

During the time Salk was working with influenza viruses, polio research had continued but with discouraging results. Thousands of new cases were reported each year, and every summer brought renewed fears of "the Crippler." By the late 1940s, a foundation set up to help polio victims and fund polio research was actively seeking more scientists to carry out projects that would lead to a prevention or cure.

As it happened, Salk was ready and available. He was looking for the opportunity to run his own laboratory, though he was not certain what specific diseases he would investigate. Salk had not studied polio intensively, but he had kept abreast of developments and discussed the disease with colleagues. His experience with viruses and vaccines had prepared him to enter polio research at this opportune moment.

FDR (seated, center) with trustees of the Warm Springs Foundation. Director Basil O'Connor stands behind Roosevelt (Roosevelt Warm Springs Institute for Rehabilitation)

The National Foundation

A unique organization to fight polio was founded almost by accident. Left paralyzed by polio in 1921, Franklin D. Roosevelt (FDR) searched for treatments that would help him to walk again. The search led him in 1924 to a thermal pool located in rural Warm Springs, Georgia. Roosevelt enjoyed swimming in the naturally warm, mineral-rich water. He could exercise longer and more productively because the buoyancy of that water helped to fight gravity.

Roosevelt decided to buy the property and run it as a combination vacation resort and treatment center. He hired health care professionals and organized card games, water basketball, picnics, musical evenings, and other activities. Polio survivors appreciated both the treatments and companionship. Some guests could not pay, but nobody was turned away. As the bills mounted, Roosevelt's law partner and friend, Basil O'Connor, suggested that Warm

Springs be run as a charitable foundation supported by grants and donations. O'Connor became executive director of the Warm Springs Foundation in 1927, and it thrived under his energetic leadership.

As president, Roosevelt continued to lend his support, and each January the foundation sponsored "President's Birthday Balls" in Washington, D.C., and around the nation. In 1934 these balls raised nearly 1 million dollars. Money was used to help polio patients around the country. The foundation paid for hospital equipment, training programs, rehabilitation centers, and other things.

In 1938 the Warm Springs Foundation became the National Foundation for Infantile Paralysis (NFIP). Americans were urged to give dimes or whatever they could afford to fight polio. After three decades of polio epidemics, people felt new hope that the disease would be conquered. They sent donations to the NFIP and even to the White House itself, sometimes taping coins onto postcards. The 1938 fund-raising drive brought in $1.8 million, even though the Depression had not ended.

To raise funds, the NFIP used modern methods of advertising and promotion. Celebrities spoke at fund-raisers and on the radio. Collection cans were passed around theaters. During World War II the NFIP organized a nationwide group of women volunteers who collected money in schools, churches, and offices. This became the annual Mother's March on Polio. Millions of dollars were raised during the 1940s. Basil O'Connor said, "The public always gives us what they think is right."

In 1941 O'Connor boldly declared that they intended to "completely eradicate the disease." The NFIP began devoting more funds to polio research. Scientists could submit their research proposals to the NFIP. Grants financed a great deal of basic research in viruses and polio.

This work continued after Roosevelt, who had been elected to an unprecedented fourth term, died on April 12, 1945, while visiting Warm Springs. Still, by the late 1940s, progress seemed slow. The NFIP had helped thousands of people to cope with polio, but there was still no cure or preventive vaccine. Some researchers had tried making vaccines but with disappointing and deadly results.

A Famous Advocate

Polio received more attention after Franklin D. Roosevelt was elected president in 1932. Roosevelt had been stricken with polio in August 1921 while vacationing at his summer home on Campobello Island, off the northeast coast of Maine. After a hectic week of traveling and outdoor activities, the 39-year-old Roosevelt experi-

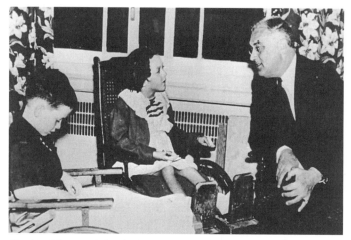

President Roosevelt inspired people with disabilities and founded the charity that became the National Foundation for Infantile Paralysis. (Roosevelt Warm Springs Institute for Rehabilitation)

Failed Vaccines

Two polio vaccines had been tested while Salk was in medical school. At the New York Health Department, Dr. Maurice Brodie and Dr. William Park made a killed-virus vaccine. They ground up the spinal cords of infected monkeys and then treated this material with the chemical formaldehyde. In Philadelphia Dr. John Kolmer made a vaccine using live but weakened viruses. Kolmer also began with spinal cord culture. Then he passed the viral material through several monkeys to weaken it. He applied two chemicals to further weaken the viruses.

enced exhaustion, fever, and a stiff neck. Then came pain, muscle weakness, and paralysis.

Roosevelt was determined to recover the use of his legs. His wealth and connections gave him access to the finest doctors and treatments. He pursued a strenuous exercise program and regained some muscle control but never walked again. Nonetheless, he resumed his political career and was invited to speak at the 1924 Democratic National Convention. People fell silent as Roosevelt entered the hall and slowly moved down the center aisle, leaning on a cane and the arm of his son Elliott. He wore his trademark broad smile, despite the strenuous effort. When Roosevelt reached the podium, the crowd gave him a thunderous ovation.

Before and during the 1920s disabilities carried a heavy stigma. In his book *FDR's Splendid Deception,* author and polio survivor Hugh Gallagher notes that people who were "severely and visibly handicapped . . . were expected to keep out of sight." With the support of family and friends, Roosevelt rejected that lifestyle. Writes Gallagher, "Roosevelt showed his party that he was, legs or no, an able contender. By doing so he helped to change the way American society viewed the handicapped, and he helped to alter the way the handicapped saw themselves."

As president, Roosevelt tackled the Great Depression with his "New Deal"—a series of progressive economic reforms and programs—and went on to lead the nation during World War II. He became a public symbol of the battle against polio and a staunch advocate for research and better treatments.

These vaccines were tested in 1935. After the Park-Brodie vaccine was administered in the fall to 9,000 people, three test subjects became paralyzed and one died. Investigators concluded that this vaccine did not protect people and might have caused their polio. Kolmer vaccinated 10,000 people. Nine children and one adult were left paralyzed, and five children died. The investigators concluded that the vaccine itself caused their deaths, probably because it did not weaken all of the viruses.

Tests on monkeys showed that neither vaccine protected them from polio. Australian virologist Sir Macfarlane Burnet offered an explanation based on his own research: There were different kinds of polioviruses, which meant that the body must be exposed to each major type before it would make antibodies against them.

The results of these failed vaccines haunted polio researchers and showed that they faced big hurdles. Nobody had found a way to culture pure polioviruses in the lab. Burnet's theory seemed plausible, and it led scientists to wonder just how many polioviruses existed. And how did they enter the body—through the nose, mouth, or other routes?

Since vaccines had not worked, researchers tried other approaches. In 1946 some of them investigated treatments that might reduce the number of viruses in the body after polio struck. None of these worked effectively. As he discussed polio research with other scientists, Salk favored the idea of a preventive vaccine. Observation had shown that almost everyone who survived polio did not get it again. They must have become immune. By the 1940s more scientists thought that a safe vaccine was feasible, despite the failures of the past. The NFIP looked for ways to make it happen.

A Lab of His Own

In 1947 the University of Pittsburgh contacted Dr. Jonas Salk. Known for its steel-making factories and the resulting pollution, Pittsburgh was changing its image. Wealthier citizens provided funds to clean up the environment and improve the city's cultural and educational facilities, including the university. At the College of Medicine Dean William McEllroy looked for promising full-time scientists to build up the research department. He offered Salk office and laboratory space in the large city-owned hospital next to the college.

The Salks moved again, this time to a rented home in Wexford, outside Pittsburgh. Salk's new lab consisted of two rooms in the basement of Municipal Hospital. Despite his meager workspace and equipment, Salk looked forward to creating a fine lab.

Recent decisions at the NFIP brought Salk squarely into the fight against polio. As director of research, Dr. Harry M. Weaver had studied the existing data and agreed there was more than one kind of poliovirus. Weaver recommended that the NFIP fund a program to count and type polioviruses. Scientists would then determine if each able to grow them in anything but nervous tissue, however, and posed problems.

That situation began to change in 1940. Drs. David Bodian and ward Howe, of Johns Hopkins University School of Medicine, e chimpanzees polio by feeding them the virus. Seven years r, researchers at Yale found that animals developed antibodies r eating polioviruses. University of Minnesota researchers then erved large amounts of virus in the feces of patients with non-alytic polio. That virus must have grown in the digestive tract. ese patients had no clear nerve damage, and such large quantities virus could not have grown solely in nerve tissue.

A huge breakthrough occurred in 1949: Three scientists at rvard-affiliated Children's Hospital in Boston grew poliovirus in nervous tissue. Drs. John Enders, Fred Robbins, and Tom Weller e conducting a five-year study of viruses funded by the NFIP. For nths, they had tested various tissue preparations and nutrient ths (liquids for cell growth) to see which broths and temperatures moted tissue growth similar to that in a live animal.

In March 1948 they decided to add poliovirus to culture flasks over from other tests. Enders had saved some frozen Lansing iovirus. Robbins later said, "I had undertaken to try cultures of use intestine, but I wasn't doing very well. I tried mumps virus on but I couldn't prove to [Enders] that I had anything. . . . He said, e been wondering about poliovirus growing in the intestine. Why n't you try it?'" Robbins tried; it did not work.

But poliovirus did grow in Weller's cultures of human muscle d skin. It multiplied in cultures that were one to three weeks old. e team tested their findings by injecting the culture fluid into the ins of mice. The mice became paralyzed. They tried diluting the id—eventually 1,000,000,000,000,000,000 times. It still caused alysis. But, as Robbins later noted, "We had to prove it three nes over before Dr. Enders would accept the fact."

The team was able to grow Lansing poliovirus in human brain d intestine. They first used tissue from the embryos of miscarried stillborn babies, since embryonic tissue grows much faster than ult tissue. Using the same methods, they also grew polioviruses on ture skin tissue. Next, they grew other strains of polio.

Jonas Salk took charge of his own lab at the University of Pittsburgh in 1947. (University of Pittsburgh, © University of Pittsburgh)

type required separate immunity or whether antibodies that fought one virus could also combat certain others. This work would require technical skills and many hours of careful observation and record keeping. The scientists also would need thousands of monkeys. Monkeys were difficult to transport, house, and handle, but they had proven most useful for polio research.

Some leading researchers declined to perform what they regarded as a menial chore. Salk, however, thought this project could help him learn more about immunology and also expand his laboratory. He later recalled his enthusiasm:

> *Weaver came along, willing to provide me with funds and work and people and facilities to be administered by me . . .*

*the virus typing work could lead to something, very much
larger. Even if it did not ... it was an opportunity to learn
something about polio, get facilities that I could do other
things with, and assemble an adequate staff.*

In Salk, the NFIP saw an energetic young virologist who had
published research papers and shown his ability to lead others.
Besides, Municipal Hospital treated polio patients and could accom-
modate the project. Weaver later said that Salk "wanted lots of space,
was perfectly comfortable with the idea of using hundreds of monkeys, and running dozens of experiments at a time. . . ." Weaver also
approved of Salk's attitude toward vaccination:

*You could talk vaccination to him without having Kolmer
and Brodie [the failed vaccines of 1935] thrown back at you.
Jonas could accept a possibility which so many old-timers
could not—that, regardless of prior theory, you might be able
to immunize human beings against polio if you put antibody
in their blood.*

The NFIP approved Salk's grant application and chose the
Pittsburgh Virus Research Laboratory as one of the four typing
teams. Each group was assigned a different part of the project, which
was expected to take two to three years. The mayor of Pittsburgh
helped by obtaining more lab space in the hospital. Salk designed
the labs himself.

The NFIP officially granted $35,900 for the work done under
Salk's direction. Later, he would receive about $200,000 to pay for
personnel, lab improvements, equipment and supplies, housing and
food for lab animals, and 30,000 test monkeys from India and the
Philippines.

An NFIP committee overseeing the typing program met in
January 1948, including Salk's mentor, Thomas Francis, who had
isolated the Mahoney (Type I) polio strain; Armstrong Lansing, who
had found a Type II strain; and Dr. John F. Kessel, who identified the
Leon strain (Type III). Another member, Albert Sabin, was a Polish-
American pediatrician known for his outstanding viral research.
During medical school Sabin had witnessed a polio epidemic in New
York City. In 1939 he accepted a position at Children's Medical

Center at the University of Cincinnati, where he began
polio vaccine six years later.

The committee discussed methods of classifying
which seemed to fall into three main types. Their plan
monkeys with known virus types, then test unknov
these monkeys and/or their blood. For example, a rese
take a monkey that had recovered from a Type I strai
it with an unknown strain to see if that virus was Type
would repeat the process to determine if the virus w
Type III. Researchers also were told to calculate the ar
needed to cause infection.

Salk preferred a reverse approach that one membe
mittee had proposed: Start by infecting monkeys v
virus types. He later said, "I saw virus classification a
logical problem, the answer to which could be found i
between virus and host, antigen and antibody. . . ." H
that some virus strains were too weak to produce v
infection. Salk wanted to type the viruses by measui
antibodies that resulted from exposure to different
way, he could determine which known virus the anti
against.

Sabin criticized Salk's proposal, and the committe
original plan. Back in the lab, Salk worked overtime s
try both approaches. The work paid off, as he later e:
typing program was to take three years, but our labo
whole thing solved before the end of the first year. E
happened during the last two years was merely confir

Crucial Discoveries

As of 1948 poliovirus was not being grown in test tub
had to obtain their virus samples from the blood and
polio patients. They then had to grow these viruses in
spinal cords of monkeys and purify them for study.
complicated process. While the typing program cor
tists learned more about how polioviruses enter the
polioviruses had been found in human feces, so scie
they might be grown in the digestive tract. For deca

The January 28, 1949, issue of *Science* heralded this discovery in an article called "Cultivation of the Lansing Strain of Poliovirus in Cultures of Various Human Embryonic Tissues" co-authored by the three scientists. Enders, Weller, and Robbins later received the 1954 Nobel Prize in physiology or medicine. The Nobel committee stated that their work "had incited a restless activity in the virus laboratories the world over."

This development was very good news for polio researchers. They could now grow large amounts of poliovirus for their studies. They would not have to wait for infected monkeys to die so they could obtain viruses from their spinal cords. Nervous tissue in a vaccine can cause allergic reactions or even death. Researchers could hope to develop a vaccine free of nervous tissue. A vaccine seemed more possible than ever before.

By summer 1950 the nation had endured decades of epidemics, and this year brought another one. For Basil O'Connor, polio hit home that summer. His daughter Bettyann O'Connor Culver, a mother of five, suffered a paralyzing attack. Therapy helped her to regain some muscle strength, but she never recovered fully. O'Connor was more determined than ever to see an end to the suffering that polio caused each year.

Pittsburgh was especially hard hit that summer. Maps in the newspapers identified places where cases of polio had been diagnosed. Each white circle indicated paralysis, while the black circles meant death. A doctor at Municipal Hospital later recalled admitting 12 children with polio in one night. Some died within hours. Others were encased in respirators that forced their limp chest muscles up and down.

Several floors below, Salk's team worked with a strong sense of purpose. They completed their typing tests, using 250 virus samples. One of Salk's chief associates was Dr. Julius Youngner, a microbiologist with experience in cancer research and cell culture techniques. He recalled, "Since we were in the same hospital with polio victims, the urgency was never out of anybody's mind."

Salk's colleagues later said that he worked tirelessly during this time and was not content unless he saw real progress. Though he was cautious, Salk also expressed confidence in his conclusions and believed that his team would succeed. The typing project was

Microbiologist Dr. Julius Youngner, at right, was a key member of the Pittsburgh research team. (University of Pittsburgh, © University of Pittsburgh)

going so well during July 1950 that Salk asked the NFIP to fund new research. He was ready to move forward with what Basil O'Connor later called "the planned miracle." One by one, Salk would tackle problems that stood in the way of a safe and effective vaccine.

Water exercises were often prescribed for people recovering from polio, but they could not reverse paralysis. (Roosevelt Warm Springs Institute for Rehabilitation)

Putting It Together

As the Pittsburgh team finished typing viruses, Salk was already conducting other studies that would help to make polio vaccine a reality. He had essential resources for developing the vaccine: ample space for research and test animals, a dedicated and capable staff, experience developing the influenza vaccine, and success in classifying polioviruses. Enders's team had overcome major hurdles by growing large numbers of polioviruses in the lab and outside the nervous system. Salk would build on that breakthrough as he looked for ways to grow larger quantities of virus. This provided material for the many experiments they would conduct in order to produce a formulation that could be tested. Salk was guided by a strong sense of purpose as he led his team through this difficult but rewarding process.

Steady Progress

The typing project, which had been designed to determine the number of polioviruses and their major groupings, yielded results. Between 1949 and 1951 Salk's Pittsburgh team "typed" 100 different viral strains. They all fell into three main types:

* Type I: 82.1 percent
* Type II: 10.2 percent
* Type III: 7.7 percent

Other teams working on the NFIP project had verified that there were indeed just three main types of polio. The NFIP was pleased, and Basil O'Connor asked Salk to undertake more research. By 1951 the two men were friends in addition to their professional relationship. They met that year onboard an ocean liner while they were both returning from a polio conference in Europe. O'Connor was impressed by Salk's knowledge and drive, as well as the consideration he showed toward O'Connor's daughter Bettyann, a polio survivor.

Team member Elsie Ward worked on various key projects while the vaccine was being developed. (University of Pittsburgh, © University of Pittsburgh)

By 1951 the NFIP was making real plans to develop polio vaccines. To show this change in focus, the Committee on Typing and Strains was renamed the Committee on Immunization. Some scientists expressed concerns based on the failed vaccines of the 1930s. Salk noted that those vaccines were designed before polioviruses were classified. Some viruses in the Park-Brodie vaccine had remained alive, while the live viruses in Kolmer's were not weakened enough to stop them from causing illness. Salk thought that the new knowledge they had acquired since 1935 would enable them to overcome these problems.

The NFIP granted Salk's request for more funding. This enabled him to buy needed lab equipment, including glass tubes and bottles and machinery. He increased his team to 50 people. The core group included Dr. Julius Youngner, Dr. L. James Lewis, and Major Byron L. Bennett. Salk added zoologist Elsie N. Ward, whose specialty was growing and maintaining live virus cultures, and Australian Dr. Percival L. Bazeley, an expert in making large quantities of pharmaceutical materials. Dr. Donald Wegemer, Dr. Ulrich Krech, and Francis Yurochko also made important contributions. Salk's lab eventually received $1.25 million of the $15 million the NFIP devoted to developing a polio vaccine.

Excited by the findings of Enders, Weller, and Robbins, Salk set out to grow polioviruses in nonnervous tissue—that is, tissue from organs outside the brain and spinal cord. Julius Youngner and Elsie Ward were assigned to that task. After experimenting with various tissues, they found that monkey kidney worked best as a medium for growing the viruses. Youngner found a way to grow even larger quantities of the virus on the same amount of tissue. He developed his own version of a technique called trypsinization, which had been developed decades earlier. Adding trypsin, a digestive enzyme that comes from the pancreas, to the tissue caused it to break down into more distinct cells where viruses could grow. Using these methods, the Pittsburgh lab was able to grow large quantities of different poliovirus strains. Salk later said, "Enders threw a long forward pass and we happened to be at a place where the ball could be caught." Youngner also developed a rapid color test to determine the amount of polioviruses in their live tissue cultures—yellow indicated the presence of antibodies while red meant no antibodies.

The virus-typing project had confirmed that an effective vaccine must contain one virus from each of the three major types. That meant that Salk's team needed to look for suitable strains from each of the three groups that would grow quickly. He later described that process:

> *Three of [the viruses] gave brilliant, startling results, destroy-ing monkey and human tissue right before our eyes. . . . These three strains, chosen at random to see how they might behave in the test tube, were obviously the best candidates for our subsequent experiments with mice and monkeys . . . and they turned out to be the strains best suited for the experimental vaccines we later tested in human beings. They were the most antigenic [causing the greatest production of antibodies] strains, the most stable, the most reliable.*

Their initial choice for a Type I virus was Brunhilde, a strain named for a chimpanzee in Howard Howe's laboratory at Yale. But this strain did not consistently promote a strong antibody response in test monkeys. Since Type I viruses caused most cases of paralysis in humans, Salk wanted a stronger immune response that would protect people. He next chose the Mahoney strain, which Thomas Francis had obtained from a family in Akron, Ohio. Although the three Mahoney children survived without paralysis, the three Kline children next door were paralyzed. For Type II, Salk selected MEF-1. Doctors working with the American Middle East Forces stationed in Egypt had obtained this strain from a British soldier in 1942. Type III was Saukett, which Salk had obtained from a paralyzed boy in Pittsburgh's Municipal Hospital in 1950. The boy's name was James Sarkett, but it was misspelled on the virus sample label.

As the Pittsburgh team moved forward, it gained a reputation for speed, efficiency, and dedication. Elsie Ward later said, "It was such pure joy to come to work . . . to look in the microscope and see what we saw was a great thrill. Dr. Salk was in the lab morning, afternoon, and night. He couldn't wait to see what was going to happen."

By 1951 Salk had helped to type polioviruses and believed that he could develop a vaccine. (University of Pittsburgh, © University of Pittsburgh)

Vaccine Debates

Some polio researchers resented Salk's expanding role, since he was less experienced and younger than many of them. He also disagreed with his colleagues about certain matters, including which type of vaccine to make. From the start, Jonas Salk favored a killed-virus vaccine over one made with weakened live viruses. Both killed- and live-virus vaccines can promote active immunity. Active immunity occurs when people make antibodies themselves. Passive immunity occurs when people receive blood serum that contains antibodies from another organism that has fought off an infection.

When disease-causing agents enter the body, a complex series of events is triggered. The body works to make antibodies for that disease. Special white blood cells called B and T lymphocytes work to disable viruses or bacteria. B cells can recognize a foreign antigen, then multiply and manufacture antibodies. The helper T cells serve to activate the B cells and other parts of the immune system. Suppressor T cells help to regulate the immune response; other T cells move additional immune cells to the infected site. Killer T cells attack and destroy foreign elements in the body, such as viruses. Still other white cells and blood substances called complement proteins aid this fight.

Vaccination gives the body a head start in this process. It forces the body to deal with an infectious agent beforehand. The white cells in the bloodstream recognize the "enemy" and send out the previously formed antibodies. Fast action can stop viruses and bacteria from multiplying, spreading, and damaging body systems.

Killed- and live-virus vaccines both aim to convince the body that an actual infection has occurred. As Edward Jenner discovered, a live virus of a mild disease (for example, cowpox) that resembles a worse one (smallpox) can achieve that goal. The outside of a cowpox virus is enough like smallpox to cause the formation of antibodies against smallpox. Unfortunately, most viral illnesses are more challenging. To cause immunity by actual infection, scientists had to find ways to attenuate—weaken—viruses, as Pasteur did with rabies.

The microorganisms in killed vaccines can no longer multiply or cause disease. Yet they can still cause antibody production if the bacterial cell walls or viral protein shells retain the structure they had when they were alive and dangerous. They are enough like their former selves to be antigenic—able to alert the body to make protective antibodies.

Salk favored a killed-virus vaccine. He found support for his ideas when he attended a conference where Dr. Isabel Morgan Mountain discussed her work on a killed-virus vaccine that prevented polio in monkeys. The monkeys' antibody levels resembled those that occur after a case of polio. This work once again confirmed the conclusion that Salk had formed during a lecture in medical school: A killed-virus vaccine could produce immunity, just as a killed-bacteria vaccine can. He and Thomas Francis proved it with their flu vaccine, and his experiments in the Pittsburgh lab showed that a preparation containing Lansing strain virus could produce antibodies in monkeys.

Salk also attended the Second International Polio Congress in Copenhagen, Denmark. John Enders told assembled scientists

Immune System Defense Mechanisms

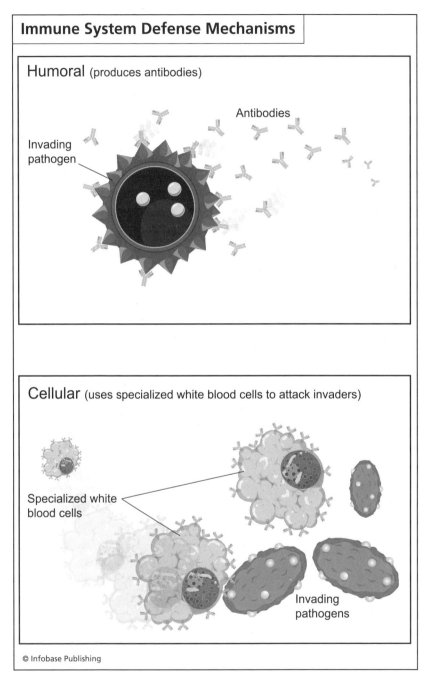

The immune system has the capacity to "recall" specific pathogens it has already encountered in the past, which triggers a defensive process against the invader.

about his tissue culture experiments. He credited Salk with show-ing that "viruses grown in test tubes could make potent animal vaccines." Salk also addressed the congress. He described his work with vaccine *adjuvants*—agents that are added to boost the immunizing power of the vaccine so that less is needed—and dis-cussed the merits of killed-virus vaccine. His presentation fueled the ongoing debate over killed-virus vaccines versus live-virus vaccines. Other scientists favored the live-virus approach. For example, Drs. Hilary Koprowski and Herald Cox were working on a live-virus vaccine for the pharmaceutical company Lederle Laboratories. They agreed with Albert Sabin that people must experience an infection, however mild, to gain lasting protection against polio.

Making either type of vaccine entailed risks. Viruses are difficult to kill. Researchers had tried using acids, phenol, and various poi-sons. Many heating and boiling processes do not kill viruses, either. Researchers had found that some preparations that were heated or treated with chemicals still caused infection.

The NFIP was now encouraging scientists to work on any prom-ising vaccine, whether live or killed. Salk believed that he was getting closer. Albert Sabin and others continued to urge caution as they continued their own research. At various meetings, Sabin warned that the human body might react quite differently to the prepara-tions than the monkeys that Salk's team was using. Salk and Sabin disagreed about numerous matters, and their conflicts would persist as both men worked on their separate vaccines.

A Hard-Working Team

As Salk and his team pressed on, they felt excited that their efforts might produce the vaccine that could help so many people. In addi-tion to guiding their scientific work, Salk aimed to keep morale high. Donald Wegemer recalled the sense of teamwork and desire to help others that motivated their work. According to Wegemer, "Salk said, 'Okay, we've got the people here who can do the job that we have in mind to do. Let's go do it.'"

Under Salk's leadership, people were working on pieces of the puzzle, both separately and in teams. Youngner and Ward were

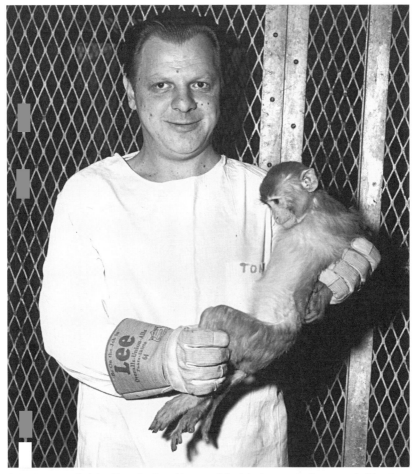

Animal care technician Tony Penka with one of the laboratory monkeys needed for the polio vaccine project (University of Pittsburgh, © University of Pittsburgh)

developing new ways to measure the levels of antibody in blood. Bennett was focusing on the inactivation process and preparation of experimental vaccines, while Lewis was responsible for the monkey studies relating to various tasks.

The team spent many hours taking kidney tissue from anesthetized monkeys. They chopped these slices of kidney tissue into tiny pieces and put the pieces into containers. Then they added a nutrient solution called Mixture 199 that Connaught Medical Laboratories, a pharmaceutical company based in Toronto, Canada, introduced in

1951. Its 62 ingredients included vitamins to keep tissue alive and penicillin, an antibiotic, to kill unwanted bacteria. Strains of poliovirus were added to the kidney cells. The viruses used the cells to

Life-Saving Machines

A severe and often deadly form of polio caused paralysis of the chest muscles. Patients who could not breathe on their own used respirators called "iron lungs," which came into use in 1928. A large electric pump changed the air pressure inside these tanks to force air in and out of the patient's lungs. The NFIP purchased iron lungs and stored them before sending them out to places where they were needed. Some polio survivors needed the "lung" for weeks, months, or years. A few people remained in them for decades and were still in iron lungs at the turn of the 21st century.

For children, an iron lung was a frightening apparatus, especially if they were seeing this machine for the first time. Besides the strange noises they made, some children thought that the people's bodies might be missing because all they could see was a head sticking out the end of the machine. Being inside the iron lung was likewise

Philip Drinker invented the first version of the iron lung. (Children's Hospital Boston, Boston, Massachusetts)

reproduce, as they would in a live organism. When Salk had a large enough sample of viruses, he tested them on mice and monkeys to see if they caused polio.

An iron lung from the 1930s (Children's Hospital Boston, Boston, Massachusetts)

terrifying, since it was an enclosed space. A patient was forced to lie there, immobilized and dependent on others for water, food, and their other needs. Without the machine, they knew that they could not even breathe. Occasionally hospitals experienced a power failure. When that happened, nurses had to pump the machines by hand.

When she was hospitalized with polio in 1952, Carol Boyer observed people in iron lungs. She later told the writer Nina Gilden Seavey " . . . that was very scary to me, to see people that had to be flat on their backs, only their heads stuck out of this big, white cylindrical machine."

Patients became familiar with the whooshing sounds of the iron lungs. At age four, Diane Kerlin, who spent nearly six months on a polio ward, could hear them from her bed. In an interview with Huntly Collins, she said, "When the nurses would turn one off, you knew that a child had died. Then they would roll the iron lung away."

Certain tests must also be done to make sure the viruses were pure (uncontaminated). If a sample tested both potent and pure, it could be used in virus-killing experiments. For killing the viruses, Salk chose *formalin,* which is made with 37 percent pure *formaldehyde.* This strong-smelling chemical disinfectant is used to preserve animal or human tissue for study in schools and laboratories. Salk and Thomas Francis had used formalin when they made their influenza vaccine.

Salk then performed numerous experiments so that he could determine how much formalin to use, how long to expose the virus to formalin, and at what temperatures. He varied the amount of formalin at different temperatures. This was called "cooking the virus," though high heat was not used. In other tests Salk varied the lengths of time from one to three weeks in this effort to determine the best blend of chemical strength, timing, and temperature. His goal was to produce a mixture in which the polioviruses were dead but still able to promote antibody production. This meant that the team must conduct many more tests on tissue cultures and the monkeys themselves to see whether or not a certain mixture gave them polio.

Salk and his staff were working long hours, often 16 hours a day, six days a week, under pressure, to make a preliminary vaccine. They moved on from working with preparations that contained one type of poliovirus to mixtures that combined three viral strains. Then began the process of subjecting these mixtures to new tests. After receiving injections of a preparation containing three polio strains, their test monkeys developed antibodies and did not come down with polio. But would this kind of preparation prevent the disease in humans? Was it safe?

The Committee Decides

The NFIP's Immunization Committee met in December 1951 to discuss vaccine-related issues. Salk gave them an up-to-date report of his experiments. He explained the process he had been using to calculate the amount of time the viruses must be exposed to formalin. For safety's sake, he explained, he then "cooked" them a few days longer.

His tests showed that no viruses remained alive, but this did not prove every virus was dead, as some committee members pointed out. No known laboratory test at the time could detect all live viruses. According to scientist John Rowan Wilson, "The ideal method of obtaining scientific data is always, of course, by direct measurement, but when for any reason this is impossible, logic and deduction have to be called into play." To visualize this process, Salk made graphs that showed a steady decline in the number of live viruses the longer they were exposed to formalin.

Salk's critics, including Sabin, claimed that these graphs did not prove every virus was dead. As the meeting continued, safety issues dominated the discussion. None of the scientists or committee members wanted to risk giving people a vaccine that could cause death or paralysis. But how could they be sure that not a single live virus remained in a vaccine? Dr. Thomas Rivers commented, "There is no test to be sure the stuff is inactive. Why not just accept that? Why kid ourselves?" Rivers suggested calling the vaccine "safe for use" rather than "inactive."

Thomas Rivers said the committee must soon decide whether or not to give Salk's preparation to humans. Sabin and his supporters argued against it. As he had done before, Sabin pointed out that the vaccine might react quite differently in human beings than in monkeys. Rivers disagreed, saying, "This is admittedly hazardous, but I am in favor of doing it as soon as possible in as cautious a manner as possible. It's time that this committee get ready to go somewhere." For years, John Enders had favored a live-virus vaccine. But now he said, "I believe in the case of this disease the possibility of using inactive vaccine is very good and one that should be very carefully explored."

The only way to find out whether the vaccine was safe was to test it. They discussed the most prudent way to begin such tests. One committee member suggested starting with people who had recovered from polio. Blood tests could be used to measure their blood antibodies both before and after they received vaccine. Salk asked the group what blood antibody level they hoped to achieve. That level could become a standard for evaluating the effectiveness of a vaccine, whether live or killed.

In the end, despite their misgivings, the committee decided to begin testing the potential vaccine on human subjects. Salk went back to his lab to prepare for these momentous first tests.

Testing the Vaccine

Once the Immunization Committee had approved the idea of testing Salk's developing vaccine, work in the lab took on even greater significance. Over the next two years, Salk moved from testing vaccine on people who had already had the disease to others who had never had polio, all the while refining the preparation and making adjustments. In between he would work on new vaccines for influenza and deal with the growing public interest in his work.

These first tests took place during years when the United States experienced the worst epidemics in its history. Once these tests were over, the committee would face another big decision—whether or not to test Salk's polio vaccine on large numbers of children on a nationwide scale.

Trial Runs

Early in 1952 Jonas Salk visited the D. T. Watson Home for Crippled Children (now the Watson Institute) in Leetsdale, Pennsylvania. He asked the directors of this respected institution to let him test his killed-virus preparation on some of the young residents. He would first test children who had already had polio, as the NFIP committee had agreed. The administrators at the Watson Home approved the plan, and the parents or guardians of 79 children let them take part. Everyone involved promised not to discuss the tests with other people or the press.

At this point the vaccine was still in a developmental stage. Salk's team was experimenting with several dozen preparations to see which might work best. Some contained one type of poliovirus, while others contained strains from all three types. Some contained adjuvant, such as mineral oil; others did not. The preparations also varied in terms of how long Salk had "cooked" the viruses. For his tests at the Watson Home, Salk intended to use three different preparations. Each contained killed viruses from one of the three polio types.

Although many researchers hesitated to go forward with human tests, Salk believed that his clear, pink-colored liquid was safe. During the 1990s, Dr. Robert Nix, the chief pediatric officer at the Watson Home, was asked if Salk was "confident in his vaccine." He replied, "Absolutely. . . . There were quite a number of people in the medical profession who were not too keen about this set up. [But] Jonas Salk knew the vaccine was good. He knew it was safe."

To begin, Salk needed to find out which types of polio each child had been exposed to. Then he would measure their blood antibodies before and after injecting his vaccine. Salk himself obtained the first blood samples. Seventeen-year-old Bill Kirkpatrick, a former high school athlete, had courageously volunteered. Wearing leg braces and a back brace, he walked toward the table with two canes. Salk withdrew his blood, saying, "Thanks for going first." Bill replied, "I have two nephews. I don't want them to get what I had." One of the other children was Jimmy Sarkett, who had been paralyzed by the strain that bore his name, misspelled as "Saukett."

The blood tests were done in the Pittsburgh lab. They showed that 60 children had antibodies against Type I polio, the most common type. These volunteers would receive a preparation containing that same type. Other volunteers would receive whatever vaccine corresponded to the type of antibody found in their blood.

On June 30, 1952, Salk returned to the Watson Home to inject killed-virus preparation into the forearms of the young volunteers. To everyone's relief, nobody became sick. His team then conducted the blood antibody tests and awaited the results. The antibodies rose just as Salk had hoped and expected they would. Six weeks later, he completed another round of injections. Salk felt some predictable anxiety during the tests, despite the care he had taken to make sure his preparation was safe. He later said, " . . . when you inoculate children with a polio vaccine, you don't sleep well for a number of months." Robert Nix later said that Salk showed "a lot of empathy" toward the children:

> . . . he would go home, and worry, and come back to the home just to check the children and see if everything was all right, that there weren't any reactions. He could have called on the phone and checked, but not Jonas. He had to come back and see it, and do it personally.

The next step was to inject children at the home who had also had polio but whose antibody levels were too low to detect. These children did not suffer any adverse effects from the vaccine either, and blood tests showed that their antibody levels rose. About seven months after the first series, Salk returned to the Watson Home to administer a final immunization shot called a booster. Tests done on the children's blood showed even higher levels of antibodies after this final injection.

By this time, people at the Watson Home were familiar with Dr. Salk and his "rattletrap car." They appreciated his kind smile and the care he took to learn their names. The cook fixed Salk's favorite strawberry pie when he was coming.

That fall Salk completed his work at the Watson Home. He prepared to conduct another series of tests, this time at a school for mentally disabled people in Polk, Pennsylvania. At this school Salk inoculated 63 people, most of them in their late teens and twenties. An epidemic of polio had swept through the region in

✦ "Please Save Our Child"

The sense of urgency escalated while Salk was testing vaccine in 1952. Polio seemed more insidious than ever. Since 1950 the number of cases had grown, hitting at least 30,000 Americans every year. Other industrialized countries also reported higher rates. For example, Britain had, on average, 4,000 cases annually. Sweden saw around 1,500, while Australia had 2,000.

The summer of 1952 brought the worst polio epidemic to date, striking new victims from Alaska to Puerto Rico and in every state, with nearly 58,000 cases nationwide. Chicago alone reported 1,203 cases, resulting in hundreds of paralyzed patients and 82 deaths. The NFIP raised $40 million that year, but it was hardly enough for such a disaster as hospitals requested more iron lungs and other equipment to meet the desperate need.

Dr. William Jordan was head of the polio unit at Case Western Reserve Hospital in Cleveland, Ohio. He recalls, "We ran out of respirators. The March of Dimes had to find some. I took care of one of our surgical residents . . . who was critically ill. . . . It was a horrible business. My own daughter got polio." Jane S. Smith writes that after that summer " . . . there was every reason to assume that the next year would be even worse, and the year after that, more terrible still. Soon, no one would be safe from the Crippler."

Pittsburgh's Municipal Hospital treated numerous polio patients. Salk's strongest motivation came from seeing the misery polio caused. His son Peter later recalled, "My father made a point of walking through that [polio] ward. People would approach him in tears. 'Please, Dr. Salk, please save our child.' There was a pathos to this, a sadness that never left his mind."

Another nurse described the human suffering:

> In all my career there has been no experience like Municipal Hospital before the Salk vaccine. One year the ambulances literally lined up outside the place. There were sixteen or seventeen new admissions every day. . . . You'd hear a child crying for someone to read his mail to him or for a drink of water or why can't she move, and you couldn't be cruel enough just to pass by. It was an atmosphere of grief, terror, and helpless rage. It was horrible.

1951, so people showed immunity to one or more polio types. For these tests, Salk combined the three types of virus in one mixture.

During these months Salk and Thomas Francis also planned to test a new flu vaccine at the University of Pittsburgh and Fort Dix, an army base in New Jersey: It contained adjuvant in the form of a mineral oil emulsion. This vaccine produced higher levels of antibodies than their previous vaccine, and the resulting immunity seemed comparable to the immunity people show after recovering from an actual attack of the flu. For Salk, this outcome bolstered his faith in the killed-virus polio vaccine.

"I've Got the Vaccine."

Salk still did not know if his vaccine would protect children who had never been exposed to live polioviruses. Neither he nor the NFIP wanted to risk deliberately infecting people to see whether or not they caught polio after receiving vaccine. Yet the results of his early

Technicians at the Pittsburgh lab are preparing tubes for color tests to check for antibodies. (University of Pittsburgh, © University of Pittsburgh)

tests were encouraging. Salk felt confident enough to tell his wife, "I've got the vaccine."

Good news came when Salk retested the antibody levels of the children he had vaccinated months earlier at the Watson Home. In the lab his team mixed samples of the children's blood with live viruses, hoping that these post-vaccination blood cells would continue to grow normally. The whole team rejoiced when that proved to be the case. Antibodies protected the cells from being destroyed by polioviruses.

That year another key question about polio was answered. Scientists feared that a vaccine would not work unless polioviruses circulated in the blood (where antibodies are located) before attacking the nervous system. Working independently, Dr. David Bodian (Johns Hopkins University) and Dorothy Horstmann (Yale University) found that polio did indeed circulate in the bloodstream after entering the digestive tract (mouth, throat, stomach, and intestines). They concluded that polioviruses entered the body by mouth and reached the blood during the early stage of infection. It reached the nervous system from five to 31 days later. This meant that antibodies in the blood could protect people from damage to the nervous system. Polioviruses would encounter blood before reaching the spinal cord and brain.

During these months Julius Youngner was working on matters relating to vaccine production and safety testing. He recalls, "Once we got momentum and it looked like we were going to be able to develop a safe vaccine, it got very exciting. You can't imagine the excitement of seeing this come to pass under your very fingers."

Salk felt confident enough to inject himself with this vaccine and then his wife and their sons: nine-year-old Peter, six-year-old Darrell, and three-year-old Jonathan. The members of the Pittsburgh lab team also received injections. Son Jonathan later said, "He knew it worked. There was no risk in his eyes. He wanted his children to be protected." Salk also believed it was not right to vaccinate other people's children if he would not vaccinate his own.

The Immunization Committee convened again in January 1953 in Hershey, Pennsylvania. Before the meeting Albert Sabin came to visit Salk's laboratory and dine with his family. The two scientists then rode together on the train to Hershey, but their professional conflicts were escalating. At the meeting Sabin insisted that it might take 10 to 15 years of testing to determine whether a polio vaccine was safe. He restated the problems of judging appropriate doses for humans based on the doses used in animals. Sabin also contended that immunity produced with a killed virus would not last long. Back in Cincinnati, he was working on his live-virus vaccine. By 1953 he was using a modified live virus that he expected would promote long-lasting immunity without causing paralysis.

The Immunization Committee debated whether or not to begin testing Salk's vaccine on large numbers of children. By this time the public was hearing rumors about the vaccine. Soon, they expected, people might start demanding it. Salk thought his team must resolve some key problems before large quantities of vaccine could be produced and injected into thousands of people. He did not want to rush into field trials too quickly.

As the NFIP discussed possible field trials, they realized that much was at stake: the integrity of the foundation, the scientists' reputations, and most important, the lives of people who would receive experimental vaccine. Dr. Thomas Rivers discussed Salk's successful tests with 161 children and pointed out, "the virus is inactivated. It is dead. . . . It is made in tissue cultures instead of brain. . . . Dr. Salk is a very cautious man. Some people want to go faster than he wants to go. Some want to throw all he has got out of the window and try something else."

When Salk spoke, he pointed out the need to look at scientific data as objectively as possible. He suggested that the committee address certain questions: Can we induce antibody formation in humans with preparations containing polioviruses that have been treated with chemicals in order to destroy their infectiousness? Is this material safe for humans, as it was for experimental animals?

Rivers asked the group, "Have we the right to wait until the ideal vaccine comes along? Should we go ahead and use this vaccine that seems to be effective right now when people are crying for it?"

For his part, Salk said that he would not yet call his preparation a "vaccine." He preferred to think in terms of preparations that had been able to induce antibody formation in human subjects.

Rivers said simply, "I think you have a vaccine, Jonas."

The Public Wants Information

After the meeting Salk returned to Pittsburgh, where he and his colleagues continued their painstaking work. Salk and his team had written a paper that was scheduled to appear in the March issue of the *Journal of the American Medical Association.* Scientists typically share their findings this way, and Salk wanted people to hear correct information, not rumors. His article discussed the results with the first 161 subjects who had been inoculated.

But news of the vaccine was leaking out. On January 26, 1953, Dr. Harry Weaver met with the NFIP's board of trustees in New York City and told them they might expect good news soon. Reporters heard about this meeting and wanted more details. By piecing bits of information together, they narrowed in on Salk and his Pittsburgh lab. An article about the vaccine and photograph of Jonas Salk appeared in the February 9th issue of *Time* magazine. The article claimed that large field trials might take place and predicted, "If the test succeeds, it will take at least another year to get mass production

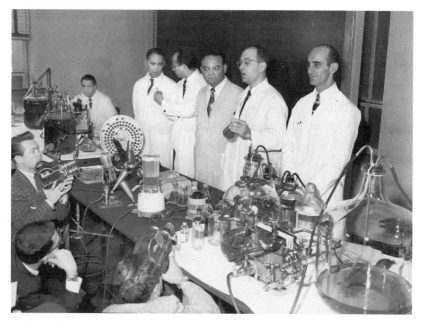

Salk and his team met with members of the press to inform them about their progress.
(University of Pittsburgh, © University of Pittsburgh)

quantities of vaccine." Unwanted publicity came from entertainment writer Earl Wilson's syndicated newspaper column, "Broadway," which appeared in newspapers around the country. Under the headline "NEW POLIO VACCINE—BIG HOPES SEEN," Wilson mentioned Salk's work. This publicity aroused even more interest, along with high expectations. People began calling the lab to request immunizations. More reporters asked Salk for interviews and photographs. Some scientists blamed Salk for the publicity and even called him a "glory hound."

Salk wanted his work described carefully and accurately in scientific journals, not gossip columns. He disliked the gossipy atmosphere that now surrounded his research. The annual March of Dimes campaign was in progress, however, and the NFIP knew that hopeful people are more likely to donate money. To give correct information and encourage favorable publicity, Basil O'Connor arranged for Salk to speak over the radio. The program, "A Scientist Speaks for Himself," was broadcast on March 26, 1953, at 10:45 P.M. O'Connor spoke first, saying,

> *You, the American people, have characteristically made yourself active partners—stockholders, if you will—in this cooperative enterprise [finding a polio vaccine] that seeks to attain better health for all the peoples of the world. . . . It's a dramatic—and inspiring—story of the contributions of many scientists in many laboratories, each playing an important part in a planned attack on polio.*

Salk then summarized the discoveries people had made during decades of polio research. In simple terms he explained how the virus was discovered, the types of polio, the history of the typing program, and the search for a vaccine. He explained the need for long-lasting protection from all three types of polioviruses. There was reason for optimism, said Salk, as scientists moved cautiously ahead. But, he added, "There will be no vaccine available for widespread use for the next polio season."

Salk impressed people during the program and the interviews that followed. Reporters noted his dark business suit and intelligent manner as he answered their questions. Salk gained their respect and affection, and some began calling him "Jonas." Fellow scientists expressed different views. Some criticized Salk for speaking to the public before his journal article appeared; others accused him of seeking publicity. To complicate matters, reporters began using the name "Salk vaccine" even though Salk called it the "Pittsburgh preparation," "killed-virus vaccine," or "poliomyelitis vaccine." He later encouraged people to use the name "Pitt vaccine" (for the University of Pittsburgh), but that name never caught on. The public and press seemed to prefer associating the vaccine with a bright, likeable hero who was out to beat polio. More publicity came after the Sunday May 31st issue of the *New York Times Magazine* featured a story announcing that "the total conquest of polio through immunization is in sight."

In the midst of these distractions, Salk and his team continued their work. They were busy checking and rechecking blood samples as they conducted new tests on monkeys. They also mixed new versions of the vaccine and analyzed them for safety. Now that success seemed imminent, the NFIP was eager to move more quickly, but Salk asked members of the Immunization Committee to be patient. He needed time to prepare and study each new batch of experimental vaccine before they offered it to the public or conducted tests with thousands of subjects.

Careful Plans

The newly formed NFIP Vaccine Advisory Committee met in May 1953 to discuss mass field trials. By then Salk had developed different batches of vaccine that could be tested on people who had never had polio or any known exposure. A doctor at the Watson Home helped him to find local families who would agree to be vaccinated. Some of these 600 people received vaccine made with mineral oil; others received a new type made with a water base. Dr. Harry Weaver and Dr. Harry Van Riper, the medical director of the NFIP, asked Salk to vaccinate their children. None of these people got polio that summer, and their blood tests showed high levels of antibodies.

During their long workdays, the Salk team continued to wonder if they had found the best way to kill polioviruses. He also wondered which mixture was superior—oil or water-base? He had to determine how many vaccinations should be given and how should they be spaced to produce optimal results. Despite some reservations, Salk agreed to proceed with mass trials. He believed the vaccine was safe, and it did produce antibodies. Yes, he could improve it, but in the meantime thousands more people could die or become paralyzed.

As the NFIP contemplated the largest medical trial in history, members felt a grave responsibility. One man on the Vaccine Advisory Committee spoke of their concerns this way: "I think the vaccine is okay. But nobody can know. What if a dozen healthy children are paralyzed?" Salk did not take part in these fateful meetings. As a final preliminary test, he immunized 5,000 children in Pittsburgh. Again, there were no incidents of polio and blood tests showed antibody formation.

In November 1953 Basil O'Connor made the long-awaited announcement: Polio vaccine trials would be held in 1954. More than a million children would take part in these first field tests, which would cost about $27 million. Heading the trials was Thomas Francis, one of the country's leading virologists and epidemiologists. People trusted Francis to conduct and evaluate the tests accurately. As he had done with the flu vaccine, Francis planned a double-blind study. Some children would receive vaccine, others a placebo. Nobody involved would know who got what until the studies ended. Code numbers on the vials would indicate to scientists which liquid was inside. A third group of children, designated as a control group, would receive nothing. When polio season arrived, scientists could measure the rates of polio in all three groups.

In choosing the sites for these trials, the NFIP picked places that had seen high rates of polio in the past. These areas seemed likely to experience similar rates again. The committee also chose places where public health departments could handle the work involved with the trials. Finally it sought to include a broad range of people from different races and ethnic groups.

For decades Americans had given time and money to defeat polio. Now they could help with vaccine trials themselves. Community volunteers organized trials in their towns and cities. Parents were asked to give permission for their children to receive the vaccine. Hospital staff gave injections at schools chosen as vaccination centers.

That fall Salk was busier than ever. He attended meetings in Detroit, Miami, New York, Washington, D.C., and other places where he presented papers and discussed the upcoming field trials. He visited Connaught Laboratories in Canada, where polioviruses were being grown to make quantities of vaccine. People continued to ask Salk for interviews, speeches, and photographs. Satisfying just some of these requests took him away from his laboratory and family. Salk valued his privacy, and his team needed to work in peace. He issued a plea to the public and media:

> *Unless we can work in the way that we see fit, uninterrupted by the many requests for material for newspaper and magazine stories, there will be insufficient time for the job that remains. . . . At the risk of seeming uncooperative I must ask that the laboratory and I be forgotten for the next six months.*

As 1954 loomed, Salk devoted much of his attention to ensuring that the vaccine was made correctly. Three different strains of viruses must be properly killed, filtered, and then combined. Safety was the foremost concern, so vaccine samples were checked three times—at the manufacturing site, at the National Institutes of Health in Bethesda, Maryland, and again in Salk's lab—to protect the children who would receive it.

"Polio Pioneers"

Polio vaccine field trials began in spring 1954. The nearly 2 million children who took part in the various control groups and experimental groups became known as Polio Pioneers. They lived in 217 health districts in 44 states. Author Jane S. Smith, then a first-grader in a New York City public school, was one of those who received the injections. She later described her experience:

> *. . . my parents signed a form which requested that I be allowed to participate in the testing of a new vaccine that might prove effective against poliomyelitis. . . . To the parents of the 1950s, there was nothing routine about polio. Everyone knew someone whose child had been stricken. . . . It's no surprise that my parents, like millions of others, gratefully volunteered their child as a test subject for Jonas Salk's polio vaccine,*

Randy Kerr, shown here with the child who represented the National Foundation for Infantile Paralysis in 1955, was the official "first" child to receive vaccine during the mass field trials. (Corbis)

disregarding any possible dangers in their desperate eagerness for protection.

The NFIP had provided training films and books for the volunteers. Besides helping with the trials, they handled piles of paperwork. Children who were not "pioneers" made name tags for the volunteers and test children. They helped to set up equipment and ran errands during the tests.

As they prepared for their injections, Smith recalls that she and her fellow Polio Pioneers felt excited. They wondered, "Where will they stick the needle? Will it hurt? Will I cry? Will I get the real stuff? Can I go swimming this summer? Does a booster shot mean they use a bigger needle?" Their teachers reassured them and explained that they were doing something brave and important.

The trials officially began on April 26, 1954, with 422,743 children aged six to nine. Cameras flashed as six-year-old Randy Kerr of McLean, Virginia, received the official first injection. Throughout America children held out their arms for either a shot of vaccine or a clear, pink liquid look-alike that was a placebo. Each child then received a lollipop and a button that read "I was a Polio Pioneer." They received three doses of vaccine (or placebo), spaced weeks apart. Another 1 million children—the control group—received nothing.

Author Jeffrey Lott was also a polio pioneer, and Salk personally gave him his vaccine. Lott recalls:

> I was part of a medical miracle. Every few weeks my classmates and I were lined up in the school gym for injections and blood tests given by researchers from the University of Pittsburgh. Like most kids I was afraid of needles, but I could tell from the way the grown-ups were acting that this was something very important. I particularly remember a balding, white-coated man named Jonas Salk, who personally injected his experimental polio vaccine into my tensed-up arm. . . . By the next spring, he was a national hero—and, visiting our school for the last time, he signed my yearbook.

In Ann Arbor, Thomas Francis organized a Vaccine Evaluation Center, where he faced the immense job of analyzing the tests. Francis and his staff assembled a full health history for every child in the three groups. They catalogued and interpreted information from the local health departments conducting the trials. This information came from mounting piles of cards, papers, letters, telegrams, laboratory reports, and health records.

As the evaluation process continued, people were eager for results. Reporters called the center for news. People wanted to know

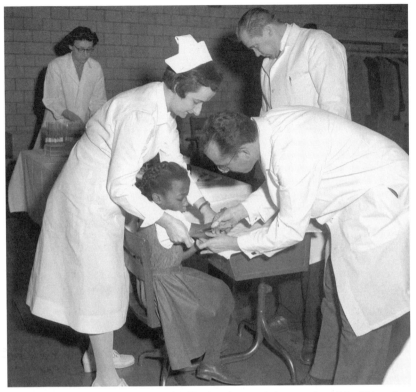

Salk helped to inoculate children in the Pittsburgh area during vaccine trials. (University of Pittsburgh, © University of Pittsburgh)

if their child had gotten "the real vaccine." Millions waited and wondered if Salk's vaccine would end 40 years of fear.

Salk himself felt confident that the vaccine would work, but the study would also give them information about how well the vaccine protected the children against the different types of polio. Salk looked forward to those results and to the culmination of these years of hard work.

7

"Thank You, Dr. Salk."

Excitement mounted both in the scientific community and among the general public during the spring of 1955 as Thomas Francis prepared to announce the results of the polio vaccine trials. Jonas Salk had worked while he waited. His lab was conducting blood tests for the trials, and Salk was looking for better ways to grow polioviruses and increase the vaccine's potency.

Once that announcement was made, Salk found himself an instant celebrity and national hero. He received numerous requests for interviews and offers to endorse commercial products. A tragedy occurred early in the national immunization program when a batch of virulent vaccine caused polio in dozens of children. This deadly accident shook public confidence and led to even stricter manufacturing and inspection procedures. As Salk dealt with these events and continued his work to improve the vaccine, he would see

Salk stands with Thomas Francis in the auditorium at the University of Michigan at Ann Arbor on the day the results of the mass field trial were announced. (Ann Arbor News)

polio rates decline as the vaccine reached millions of Americans and people in other countries.

A Historic Announcement

Thomas Francis was ready to announce the results of the field trials at the University of Michigan. More than 500 people, including government and public health officials, NFIP administrators, scientists, physicians, and journalists, were invited to the auditorium there. Jonas Salk brought Donna and their sons to Ann Arbor. He was eager to include his family, who had made many sacrifices during his years of research. His younger brother, Lee Salk, also attended the meeting. Their parents could not make the trip, but they joined a group watching the report on television at a large New York hotel.

On the morning of April 12 Salk was seated onstage between Thomas Francis and Basil O'Connor. Francis rose to speak at 10:20 A.M., and radio and television stations prepared to broadcast the news. Reporters inside the pressroom were already scanning their written reports. Excited cheers rang out as they read certain key phrases: "The vaccine works. It is safe, effective, and potent."

Francis used these same words as he summarized the results of the field tests for the assembled guests. He declared that the vaccine was 100 percent effective against Type II and 92 percent effective against Type III polio. It was somewhat less effective—68 percent—against Type I. It was about 94 percent effective against the rare type of polio that paralyzed breathing muscles. Among vaccinated children living in epidemic areas, rates of polio were 50 percent lower than among unvaccinated children. None of the children who received vaccine had gotten polio as a result.

At first people remained silent as they absorbed this momentous news. Author Jeffrey Kluger describes the special silence in Rackham Hall that day:

> [It was] filled with a noisy uncoiling . . . the uncoiling of a spring that had been wound tight since 1916 when 9,300 boys and girls in New York City were claimed by [polio]. It was a spring that had been wound since 1935, when 19,000 children had consumed a bad vaccine and waited to see if it would save them or kill them. It was a spring that had been wound since 1952, when 57,879 children were inked into the virus-counter's casebook.

Some people in the audience wept as Francis spoke for one hour and 38 minutes, showing charts and graphs to illustrate the statistics. David Bodian spoke next. He discussed polio research and the contributions of many scientists. He was followed by Thomas Rivers and then Basil O'Connor, who talked about Franklin Roosevelt and the history of the NFIP. O'Connor acknowledged the millions of Americans who had donated time and money to fight polio.

Cameras flashed and people rose to applaud as Jonas Salk took the microphone. Salk had believed the vaccine would work—his data and cultures had told him so. Now rigorous testing had produced statistics that supported his theories and vindicated his faith in the vaccine. He had even more reasons to feel confident, because his team had developed an improved version. He had found that lengthening the time between the second and third injections also enhanced its performance.

As he began to speak, Salk thanked the NFIP leaders, the children of the Polk School and Watson Home, and the Polio Pioneers. He mentioned scientists whose work paved the way for the vaccine. However, he did not thank each member of the Pittsburgh Virus Research Team by name. Instead, he thanked them as a group, saying, "I can speak of what they have done and repeat that they, as I have said of Basil O'Connor, can enjoy 'the reward of a thing well done' not only from having done it but, I hope, their reward will come, too, from being able to do more." He then discussed their ongoing work with the vaccine.

For years to come, Salk would be criticized for not thanking his associates individually, especially Julius S. Youngner, Byron L. Bennett, and the other team members who had made major contributions. Thomas Francis thought that Salk also should not have discussed improved methods of vaccination at the meeting held to report on the existing vaccine. Other critics accused Salk of wanting too much credit for himself, even though he did not give himself credit at the meeting either.

The name of the vaccine remained controversial. At the press conference Salk said that if anyone's name were used, it should be Basil O'Connor's. People continued to call it "Salk vaccine," however.

Removed from these scientific debates, the general public felt joy and relief. Factory sirens were sounded and trolley bells rang. Shoppers cheered as store loudspeakers repeated the announcement. People laughed, wept, and embraced on the streets. Schools closed early. Some towns organized public celebrations. A realtor in New Jersey painted the words "Thank you, Dr. Salk" in large letters on his store window.

Polio vaccine was front-page news. Repeating Francis's words, headlines read: THE SALK VACCINE IS SAFE, EFFECTIVE, AND POTENT. Others announced, POLIO CONQUERED! or POLIO ROUTED! The U.S. secretary of health, education, and welfare, Oveta Culp Hobby, said, "It is a wonderful day—for the whole world." The

April 25th issue of *Newsweek* ran an article entitled "A Quiet Young Man's Magnificent Victory" and declared, "The Crippler had finally been beaten."

Celebrity Status

When the Salks returned to Pittsburgh, hundreds of people greeted them at the airport. Police escorted them home and patrolled their street. Both at home and in the lab, Salk was deluged with phone calls, telegrams, and sacks of mail. Some letters contained checks or cash. People also sent gifts, including cars. Salk announced that he was giving these things to the NFIP. His family obtained an unlisted telephone number to protect their privacy.

At age 40 Jonas Salk was famous. People wanted more information about his work and his personal life. Reporters clamored for photos and interviews and called Salk a savior, benefactor of mankind, genius, and hero. Members of Congress suggested minting a new dime with his image, and streets and schools were renamed for him. When movie studios asked to make a film about his life, Salk refused, saying that such films were best made after their subjects died. Showing a wry sense of humor, he said, "I am willing to await my chances of such attention at that time."

Although he mentioned other people's contributions to the vaccine, Salk continued to receive the credit. The media called him "the man who conquered polio." In countless interviews, Salk answered questions and discussed medical research and disease prevention. While some scientists criticized his fame, others praised Salk's poise and communication skills. They said that he represented their community well and helped people learn more about science.

During these months Salk often traveled to New York City and Washington, D.C. He attended conferences and met with health officials, NFIP leaders, and drug manufacturers. He wanted more time in the laboratory, but the demands on his time persisted throughout 1955. Salk later said, "I suddenly found myself being treated like a public figure, a hero. I was no longer able to use my time altogether at my own discretion . . ."

On April 22, a special ceremony was held in the Rose Garden at the White House. President Dwight D. Eisenhower presented

Salk and Basil O'Connor with the U.S. Medal of Merit. Eisenhower seemed moved to tears as he expressed gratitude that his grandchildren could be protected from polio. Although Salk was asked not to make a speech, he insisted that he must mention other scientists who developed the vaccine, especially his Pittsburgh team. Salk accepted the medal "on behalf of all the people, in laboratories, in the field and those behind the lines."

Many other honors followed, including the Albert Lasker Award and the Criss Award. Salk told friends that he was embarrassed by what he later called "an inordinate amount of recognition and attention." He did not attend every ceremony. To shift the focus, he asked polio pioneers to accept some awards in his place. More and more he understood what journalist Edward R. Murrow meant during the television interview they had done together when Murrow said, "Young man, a great tragedy has just befallen you. You've just lost your anonymity."

Salk received lucrative offers to endorse products or other commercial ventures. One company wanted to market children's pajamas bearing his name. People respected Salk for declining these offers and for his comments during the interview with Edward R. Murrow. When Murrow asked him who owned the patent to the polio vaccine, Salk replied, "Well, the people I guess. There is no patent. Could you patent the sun?"

Mass Immunizations

Once the vaccine was licensed for use, public demand soared. At first government officials assumed that private physicians would handle polio vaccinations. Together with the NFIP, they then decided that all children should be vaccinated. This meant that large quantities of vaccine must be quickly produced, inspected, and distributed. The NFIP had negotiated with six drug manufacturers that were making large quantities of polio vaccine. The NFIP and the U.S. Department of Health, Education and Welfare had not expected such massive demand immediately after the April 12th announcement, however.

The problems of shifting to large-scale production led to a tragedy. On April 24 a doctor in Idaho reported that a child developed polio six days after being vaccinated. She died three days later. By then, other cases had occurred among vaccinated children. On April 25, a baby was rushed to the emergency room of a Chicago hospital. Nine other cases of paralysis among vaccinated people were reported in California, Georgia, and Idaho.

The U.S. surgeon general and other officials were informed. Basil O'Connor and Jonas Salk met with members of the U.S. Public Health Service to determine what had gone wrong. The newly organized polio surveillance unit of the Epidemic Intelligence Service (EIS) of the Centers for Disease Control (CDC) went to work. This unit included only three people: 28-year-old Neal Nathanson, M.D., a statistician, and a secretary. Investigators found that, in the first 10 cases of paralysis that were reported, the vaccine came from Cutter Laboratories in California.

More cases of polio were reported and by April 29 six states had found 26 cases of polio among vaccinated children. Some cities cancelled their vaccination programs, but a million doses already had been given. On May 7 the number of casualties rose to 44, and the government halted the entire program.

Investigators needed answers. They had to determine if these were cases of polio that the vaccine had failed to prevent, or if the vaccine was responsible—meaning that some viruses remained alive. If one manufacturer had produced all the faulty vaccine, that might indicate they had not made it properly. If more than one company produced faulty vaccine, the vaccine recipe might be the problem.

The CDC set out to identify all polio cases linked to a vaccination. Using a detailed questionnaire, they interviewed hundreds of investigators and public health personnel all over the country. Nathanson later recalled, "We worked from seven in the morning till nine at night. We'd go home and drop, and start again the next morning."

The public felt confused and fearful in the meantime. In an article published on May 13, the *New York Times* reported that "the nation is now badly scared. . . . Millions of parents fear that if their children don't get the vaccine they may get polio, but if they do get the vaccine, it might give them polio."

Investigators made progress after they found that Idaho had far more cases of polio than usual for April. Idaho had received a large share of Cutter vaccine, as had the company's home state, California.

In most victims the paralysis began in the limb that received the injection. This was another clue that vaccine caused their polio. When polio began naturally, the disease would start in the legs and move upward. Inspectors found live poliovirus in vaccine samples at the Cutter plant. On May 24, the U.S. surgeon general announced that two lots of Cutter vaccine had been removed from the program. Other lots would not be used until inspectors examined and approved them. Five successive runs must test as safe before vaccine was released.

The Cutter case revealed problems in manufacturing large batches. Formalin disabled poliovirus by coagulating the proteins on its surface, which prevented the virus from attaching to cells. The coagulation process caused the proteins to become sticky. As a result, nearby viruses in the vaccine solution could clump together. Sometimes live virus particles survived in these clumps. Clumping was visible when making small batches, because sediment sank to the bottom of the glass containers. Vaccine manufacturers were filtering the vaccine. But it seemed that at the Cutter plant some had slipped through during mass production. The vaccine may have sat for too long between the time it was filtered and the time it was "cooked." This would allow more sediment to form.

To address these problems, Salk worked with health officials to provide even more detailed guidelines for making polio vaccine. New regulations required manufacturers to filter the viral material both before and during the time it was in formalin. The U.S. Public Health Service also resumed checking the vaccine, as it did for the field trials.

Eventually, 79 vaccinated children became ill, and they spread polio to friends and family members. According to a report later issued by David Bodian, 200 people suffered permanent paralysis and 11 died. In later years the Cutter Company faced lawsuits claiming negligence, and Salk testified on behalf of the affected families. He was devastated that people were harmed by the vaccine. Salk told a friend, " . . . I cannot escape a terrible feeling of identification with these people who got polio."

The Cutter incident hurt Salk's reputation, because he had reassured people the vaccine was safe. Many people did not understand what went wrong. Basil O'Connor worked to restore confidence by

Dr. Albert Sabin developed an oral version of polio vaccine. (Photo Researchers)

explaining that new safety measures were in place. He claimed that anyone who blocked people from being vaccinated "must be prepared to be haunted for life by the crippled bodies of little children who could have been saved from paralysis had they been permitted to receive the Salk vaccine."

Others advocated an end to the mass immunizations. They included the American Medical Association (AMA). At its annual convention in June the AMA passed a resolution objecting to free, mass vaccinations and government involvement in the delivery of medical services. The AMA proposed treating polio vaccine like other drugs and vaccines. They said it should be free only for people who could not afford it, and others should obtain it from their physicians. Albert Sabin said the program should be stopped. He also suggested replacing the Mahoney strain with a different Type I strain that was less virulent. The NFIP Vaccine Committee agreed that this suggestion should be implemented, but it did not halt the immunization program.

By the end of 1955, about 7 million American children had received at least one dose. No new cases of polio were linked to the vaccine. Around the world, an additional 7.5 million children received Salk's vaccine. The rate of polio for 1955 fell by 25 percent below the five-year average. Once polio season ended, the government set up even stricter standards for filtering vaccine to prevent clumping of virus particles. For added safety, monkeys were given cortisone before the vaccine was tested on them. Cortisone made them more prone to infection, which meant that even tiny amounts of live virus could give them polio.

Polio Rates Decline

Salk hoped that polio rates would continue to decline as more Americans received their vaccinations. By 1956 about 30 million Americans had been vaccinated. Congress had allotted $30 million for the program, but the states had used less than $10 million. Some observers said they were responding to pressure from the AMA, which continued to oppose mass vaccinations. That summer 1,100 cases of polio were reported in Chicago, where the AMA is headquartered.

In response to this situation, Salk wrote to the U.S. surgeon general, who approved of the mass vaccinations. Salk noted that some shipments of vaccine were being returned, unused, from state distribution sites, although polio season had arrived. Salk urged the surgeon general to publicly support vaccination. The NFIP also continued to encourage vaccinations. Just 9 million Americans had received all three injections, which meant the vaccine was not reaching as many people as the NFIP hoped. Still, the incidence of polio had declined nearly 61 percent in two years with 15,140 cases reported in 1956.

Two groups of physicians, the American Academy of Pediatrics and the American Academy of General Practice, did support the program, and the AMA changed its position somewhat in 1957. Salk spoke at their annual convention, saying that a sense of social responsibility was needed to defeat polio. The AMA did not fully support mass vaccinations, but stated that the polio vaccine might as well be used because so much effort and money went into developing it and it seemed to be effective.

By the end of 1957 about 50 percent of all Americans under age 40 had received all three doses of vaccine. That year 5,787 cases of polio were reported. This was 86 percent below 1950–54 levels. Critics still did not credit Salk's vaccine for the declining rates, however. They said that polio cycles changed from year to year and these lower rates might be a coincidence.

POLIO IN THE UNITED STATES

Year	Number of polio cases reported in the United States
1954	38,478
1955	28,985
1956	15,140
1957	5,485
1958	5,787
1959	8,425
1960	3,190
1961	1,312
1962	910

Statistics from the U.S. Department of Health & Human Services, Public Health Service, Centers for Disease Control

Statistics showed researchers that polio was more common in low-income neighborhoods, especially among minorities with low vaccination rates. This happened in Chicago in 1956 and Washington, D.C., in 1957. Across the country unvaccinated white Americans had lower rates of polio than unvaccinated African Americans. Scientists claimed that people living in areas with low vaccination rates were exposed to polio more often. A larger group of "unprotected" people could spread more viruses. Epidemiologists call this a "chain of transmission." Increasing the number of vaccinated people in a community reduces the number of disease carriers. In 1959 polio epidemics struck Kansas City, Missouri, and Des Moines, Iowa. Scientists noticed a pattern like the one they had seen in 1956 and 1957. In Kansas City, more African Americans than whites got polio. Five years earlier the reverse had been true. To prevent these cases of polio, Salk urged the government to make sure all Americans were immunized, regardless of their ability to pay.

Other countries, including Great Britain, had begun using the Salk vaccine. In 1955 the United States exported small amounts. It shipped 3 million doses to Poland when an epidemic broke out there in 1958. That same year it shipped three tons to Hungary. A British-made vaccine became available during the late 1950s. It was limited to younger citizens until more vaccine was available. People over age 40 were not vaccinated until 1960.

By 1959 more than 90 countries had received some Salk vaccine. The World Health Organization (WHO) studied the effects of vaccination programs in Canada, South Africa, France, Germany, Sweden, and Denmark. They saw declining rates of polio. In the United States rates continued to decline. There were 3,190 cases in 1960.

To Salk's relief, there were no further disasters like the Cutter incident. He watched the polio statistics closely after his vaccine came into use. By 1960 he could point to objective evidence that his killed-virus vaccine did indeed prevent polio. Though he would continue to work with polio-related issues, he was embarking on some exciting new ventures.

Opportunity to "Do More"

Despite the many demands on his time after April 1955, Jonas Salk returned to his laboratory, planning to conduct basic research in virology and immunology. He continued to improve the killed-virus vaccine and worked with agencies and organizations trying to defeat polio around the world.

During his speech at Ann Arbor, Salk had noted that one great benefit of success is the chance to "do more." At age 40, Salk was still young, with a long list of new goals he hoped to achieve. His fame had brought many unwelcome consequences, but it also brought him opportunity, which he used to fulfill his vision for a world-class scientific institute that would facilitate his work and the work of other scientists.

Planning a Unique Institute

Though Salk attempted to return to work with minimal publicity, people continued to wonder what he was doing, and journalists followed his activities. When the Pittsburgh laboratory began cancer research in 1956, the public hoped—and perhaps expected—that Jonas Salk could conquer any disease he studied. A 1958 survey showed that Salk was one of the two best-known American scientists. The other was physicist Robert Oppenheimer, who directed the secret research project to build the atomic bomb during World War II.

In 1957 Salk's title at the university was changed to Commonwealth Professor of Experimental Medicine. He was increasingly frustrated by the amount of time he spent on administrative duties. Some of the diseases that interested him, such as cancer and multiple sclerosis, were highly complex. They would require decades of intensive study and collaboration with other scientists. He later said, "I was an immunologist and my first interest was in experimental medicine—life, people, ideas. I wanted an unstructured situation where almost anything would be possible. The world was open. Knowledge was expanding. I wanted to be in the thick of things."

As he looked ahead, Salk envisioned a new kind of scientific institute where brilliant scientists and scholars could work on projects of their choice in a stimulating research community. The ultimate goal of their work would be to improve the quality of human life. Salk was excited by what he called "the possibility of bringing together leading workers in diverse fields and freeing them to collaborate with each other without departmental or administrative barriers." He thought that traditional divisions among disciplines could block the flow of information and ideas. Creativity and insights are more likely to thrive, said Salk, when people connect. Salk planned to invite people from other disciplines, including sociology, history, and philosophy, to add knowledge about human behavior that could promote health in the broadest sense of the word.

These attitudes had begun forming in Salk's youth, when he wanted to examine ideas and problems in a fresh, individual way. He had never found an ideal setting for this kind of research. Now perhaps he could create one? In such a setting he could pursue his

An Expanding Organization

In 1958 the NFIP declared that polio was no longer a major health threat. The Salk vaccine had achieved its goal, and the NFIP stopped funding polio research. From then on they were called simply the National Foundation, later changed to the March of Dimes. The organization had made history as the first charitable organization to care for victims of a specific disease while funding research to fight that disease. It also pioneered the idea of organizing volunteers across the nation.

The March of Dimes continued to help people with polio-related problems but shifted its focus to arthritis and birth defects. Today it devotes considerable resources to promoting the health of mothers and babies worldwide in order to prevent problems associated with premature birth and low-birth weight. This includes funding research to study genetic birth defects, such as hemophilia.

The March of Dimes continues to help people who survived polio. An estimated 1.1 million people in the United States alone were stricken with polio after 1940. Some were left with serious disabilities, and a few remained respirator-dependent as of 2006. In 2000 the March of Dimes cosponsored a global symposium on post-polio syndrome, a condition that afflicts many survivors. Some began to experience symptoms decades after they recovered from the disease. These symptoms include fatigue, pain, and weak muscles in body parts that have worked extra hard to compensate for polio-related damage. At the conference, which was held at the Warm Springs Rehabilitation Center in Georgia, people discussed ways to cope with the physical and emotional impact of post-polio syndrome. The March of Dimes continues to publish and distribute information to help health care professionals and people with post-polio syndrome cope with this condition. Since 2005, to mark the 50th anniversary of the announcement about the polio vaccine, the organization has sponsored a forum on its Web site called "Share Your Story" for polio survivors, polio volunteers, and polio pioneers.

work and live more privately. He shared this vision at a scientific conference in New York City in 1957:

The time is drawing to a close when one can hope to find full understanding of many more disease processes through one discipline alone. . . . There are many viewpoints and areas of interest and there are differences in techniques used by the physicist, the chemist, the biologist, the physician, and the epidemiologist. Where cause and effect relationships are not clearly apparent, new insights come either from probing more deeply or from looking at the familiar from the unfamiliar viewpoint of another discipline.

In March 1960 officials at the University of Pittsburgh announced that Jonas Salk was leaving. People who knew and admired him as Pittsburgh's most famous citizen were sorry to see him go.

A Dream Fulfilled

Salk worked for several years to make the scientific institute a reality. During that time, he wrote copious notes and sketched some of his ideas for designing the facilities. He first considered locating the institute on the University of Pittsburgh campus, but could not reach an agreement with university officials. They wanted some control over the facility, and Salk wanted autonomy.

Basil O'Connor, his loyal supporter, offered to help Salk raise money. About $20 million of the initial funding came from the National Foundation/March of Dimes. O'Connor expressed confidence that Salk would assemble a distinguished group of scientists. The knowledge coming from the institute could benefit the March of Dimes, which was now focusing on preventing and treating birth defects. Other funding for Salk's institute would come from research grants, the National Institutes of Health, and private individuals and organizations.

Salk wanted the building and its surroundings to "evoke and inspire creativity." In 1959 he visited San Diego and met Mayor Charles Dail, who had been crippled by polio. Dail asked the city to donate coastal land along Torrey Pines mesa in La Jolla, near the University of California at San Diego, for Salk's use. Some local residents objected. They said that infected lab animals might pose problems and large buildings could mar the landscape. The plan was approved, however.

As Salk headed west in 1960, he looked forward to designing the institute and choosing the people who would work there. It was a huge project, but he anticipated great rewards in "having a place where science and philosophy and human values and the significant in life are artistically combined in a new synthesis that will live and grow . . . "

It would start with the building. Salk found a famous architect who shared his vision: Philadelphia architect and artist Louis I. Kahn. Kahn designed the buildings, set on 26 acres overlooking the ocean, and construction began in 1962. His innovative yet simple design has been called an architectural masterpiece. Photos of the Salk Institute appear in books and textbooks about architecture and architectural history. Salk and Kahn worked to design interior spaces that would function well for research purposes, aiming for spaces that were inspiring both inside and out.

With Salk as its first president, the Salk Institute for Biological Studies was officially founded as a private, nonprofit facility in 1963. The buildings were still being constructed, so people began working in temporary offices. Salk resigned as president of the institute

The Salk Institute for Biological Studies is a world-famous scientific research facility. (Corbis)

in 1965 to serve as director, focusing his attentions on research and academic development. Two years later, the core building was finally completed. During these hectic years Salk again gave up time in the lab so that he could organize and direct the institute. He said that this tradeoff brought him satisfaction in producing "not just a new lab but a dynamic new setting—and not just for myself but for some of the most productive and imaginative biological scientists in the world."

The Sabin Vaccine

While Salk was developing the institute, the Sabin polio vaccine came into use. Albert Sabin had first tested his vaccine, which used the live-attenuated virus approach, in the former Soviet Union. Polio had been rising in the Soviet Union since 1954, with an average of 18,000 to 20,000 paralytic cases annually. Since people in the United States and Europe were already using Salk's vaccine, Sabin looked for another place to conduct a field test, and the Soviet Union was willing to take part. By 1960 millions of Russians had taken three doses of Sabin's vaccine, which was given orally, not by injection. Each dose contained one type of poliovirus. Manufacturers had not yet found a way to combine all three types in one dose. Sabin went on to test his vaccine in the former Czechoslovakia and Singapore. Based on these tests, it appeared to be safe.

In 1961 U.S. government officials approved Sabin's vaccine for use and licensed the Type I and Type II. Type III was approved the following spring. For the first time in its history, the AMA approved the vaccine before it was released. Some people claimed that the AMA favored Sabin's vaccine because it used the traditional live-virus approach and was easier to take, since it was swallowed on a lump of sugar. Sabin's vaccine was also less expensive than injected vaccine.

Critics expressed their concerns. They noted that tamed, or attenuated, viruses can return to a wild state while passing from person to person. Some worried that the Type II virus in the vaccine might be unstable. Live viruses keep growing, reproducing, and changing. What would happen to the vaccine as it moved from the digestive tract to the blood and central nervous system? Critics also noted that doses of Sabin vaccine were spaced four to six weeks apart, but people sometimes missed getting one or more of the doses on the scheduled date. Missed doses might cause unpredictable interactions among the viruses, warned critics.

Salk actively joined this debate, contending that the push to use oral vaccine was unreasonable and premature. He suggested that health authorities first ensure that all younger Americans received killed-virus (also called inactivated) vaccine. Polio rates had steadily declined since 1955, but the vaccine could not eliminate polio unless it reached enough people. Salk later said, "In a sense our field trial of the inactivated vaccine principle was still in progress. We knew that, if the other vaccine were kept out of the community until the end of 1961, the decreasing incidence statistics would be inescapable proof that the inactivated vaccine could eradicate polio."

As a compromise, some scientists suggested that oral vaccine be introduced quickly in countries where injected killed-virus vaccine had never been widely used. It might not be necessary in the United States or other countries where people had been using the Salk inactivated polio vaccine successfully.

Within a few years, however, Sabin's became the vaccine of choice in the United States. April 24, 1960, known as "Sabin Oral Sunday," marked the first day that people in the United States received Sabin's vaccine. As of 1961 communities throughout the country were holding SOS—Sabin Oral Sunday—campaigns, and people lined up at schools or other places to receive their vaccine on a sugar cube. Local officials and medical societies encouraged people to take oral vaccine, even if they were already vaccinated by injection. The SOS campaigns were publicized in the newspapers, on billboards, and by bus drivers and others who wore "SOS" buttons. Large cities operated numerous vaccination stations. For instance, during an SOS day in 1962 people in Cleveland could go to one of 92 centers. By 1963 Sabin vaccine was more widely used than Salk's.

Polio rates continued to drop while the debates over the two vaccines went on. Statistics gathered in 1961 showed that polio had declined in America by 97 percent compared to the average rates from 1950–54. Only 910 cases were reported in 1962. Basil O'Connor and others noted these declining rates and attributed them to Salk's vaccine. They questioned why the United Public Health Service, the AMA, and various drug companies were promoting Sabin's vaccine.

As of mid-1964, about 100 million Americans had taken three doses of oral vaccine. Most paid the 25-cent fee that was requested but not required. Problems arose in June 1964 when 123 cases of paralytic polio were reported among people who had received oral vaccine in May. The U.S. Public Health Service found that 57 cases resulted from the vaccine; 36 were uncertain. To advocates of the killed-virus approach, these cases of polio showed the dangers of using a vaccine with weakened, not killed, viruses. Salk continued to advocate killed-virus vaccine as the safer approach.

Excluding those 123 cases, only 35 reports of polio occurred during the first six months of 1964. This was significantly lower than the annual average of 16,316 cases during the early 1950s. The use of Salk's vaccine, beginning in 1955, seemed like the logical explanation for the decline of polio. In 1965 the U.S. Senate and House of Representatives passed a joint resolution expressing the nation's gratitude to Jonas Salk and the National Foundation on the 10th anniversary of the announcement at Ann Arbor.

Sabin's vaccine became the norm in most countries, but a few, including the Netherlands and Scandinavian nations, continued to use killed-virus (inactivated) vaccine. No cases of paralytic polio were reported in those countries after 1962. In the United States doctors sometimes opted to use killed-virus vaccine for people with weakened immune systems. This lowered their risk of contracting polio from viruses that were weakened but not dead. The debate over the two vaccines continued for decades, with Salk and Sabin continuing to defend their different approaches.

Great Minds Gather

Salk spent the early 1960s building up the scientific institute with the energy and care that he applied to his research. From the beginning, the people in residence included Nobel laureates and members of prestigious scientific societies, such as the National Academy of Sciences and the Royal Academy of London. Ten prominent men accepted Salk's invitation to join him in La Jolla. Five of them held the title of resident fellow and faculty member:

* Mathematician-philosopher Jacob Bronowski had written a report about the devastating effect of atomic bombs on Hiroshima and Nagasaki in Japan.

* Renato Dulbecco, a versatile physician, bacteriologist, virologist, geneticist, and physicist, specialized in viruses and cancer. He would receive a Nobel Prize in physiology or medicine in 1975 for his work.

* Edwin Lennox had been part of the theoretical physics division for the Manhattan Project to build the atomic bomb.

* Biochemist Melvin Cohn specialized in immunology.

* Chemist Leslie E. Orgel focused on genetics and the origins of life on Earth.

Another five scientists became nonresident fellows:

* Salvador E. Luria, a pioneering microbial geneticist, was part of a team that won the 1969 Nobel Prize in physiology or medicine for their work on the replication and genetic structure of viruses.

* Jacques Monod, another geneticist, worked with a team that won the 1965 Nobel Prize in physiology or medicine for their discovery of the genetic control over production of proteins and enzymes.

* Warren Weaver, an eminent science administrator brought expertise in engineering and mathematical physics. Weaver is credited with coining the term *molecular biology* in 1938.

* British physicist Francis H. C. Crick had collaborated with Maurice Wilkins and James D. Watson to discover the structure of the DNA molecule, for which they received the 1962 Nobel Prize in physiology or medicine. The DNA molecule contains the genetic code that transmits the traits for all living things.

Salk also invited his friend Leo Szilard, a Hungarian-American who had played a key role in the Manhattan Project to build the atomic bomb during World War II. Szilard, a physicist and biologist, had encouraged Salk to found the institute. He himself died a few months after he arrived in 1964.

Salk Institute fellow Francis Crick (at right) with his colleague James D. Watson and their model of the DNA molecule (Photo Researchers)

By 1968 140 people were working at the institute, and most of them were involved in research. Salk later said that choosing these first scientists was just the beginning of an "evolutionary process" that would continue to attract people of quality. The institute, he hoped, would continue its work long into the future.

Besides his scientific and administrative roles, Salk was writing and teaching. He had been appointed adjunct professor in health sciences at the University of California at San Diego. In his own laboratory Salk was focusing on studies of immunology, cancer, and autoimmune diseases. Autoimmune diseases come from inside, not outside, the body. Some examples are allergies, thyroid disease, arthritis, myasthenia gravis (in which important proteins in muscle tissues are destroyed), and multiple sclerosis (in which the body attacks the protective sheath on its own nerve cells). Autoimmune responses occur when the body mistakes its own cells for a foreign organism and produces antibodies against them. These antibodies then destroy healthy cells, causing various symptoms and health problems.

In 1968 Donna and Jonas Salk were divorced. Donna Salk had not enjoyed the public attention and numerous social events that came with her husband's fame and position. She had maintained her professional interests while rearing their three sons and managing the household. After the divorce she remained in San Diego and resumed her career as a social worker.

Jonas Salk remarried in 1970. He had met his new wife, French-born artist Françoise Gilot, the previous year while she was visiting San Diego. Salk gave her a tour of the institute, and they discovered many shared interests. Gilot had studied law, philosophy, and literature, as well as art. She had lived with the legendary artist Pablo Picasso from 1944 to 1953, and they had two children, Paloma and Claude.

Along with these personal changes came some professional changes. In 1972 Salk decided to shift his role at the institute. He would keep the title of director but no longer had the responsibility for administrative duties. This gave Salk more time for research as well as more time for humanitarian activities. Salk's title at the institute would change again in 1975 to that of founding director.

Toward a Better World

Salk used his platform as a well-known and respected scientist to influence matters concerning public health. He continued to speak out, especially on matters that affected children. He became concerned in 1968 when researcher Dr. Dorothy M. Horstmann observed that children in low-income homes were not receiving all the vaccinations that pediatricians recommended. This trend had begun after the Federal Vaccination Act of 1962 ended. The act gave state and local health departments funds to help pay for vaccinations. Horstmann wrote, "The U.S. Immunization survey reveals a steady fall in the past few years in the percentage of children immunized against poliomyelitis and measles, particularly among the urban poor." Salk joined Horstmann and others who warned that polio and other diseases could spread in places where children were not vaccinated. Salk urged people to receive important immunizations.

The 1970s found Salk again working on polio vaccines. An enhanced version of inactivated vaccine became available in 1977. This version produced immunity with only one or two doses. It could be mixed with certain other vaccines, which made the immunization process more efficient. Salk consulted with the laboratories in Canada, France, and the Netherlands that collaborated to develop this vaccine.

During this decade Salk also spent more time writing. He examined global problems in ways that blended his scientific and philosophical thinking. *Man Unfolding* was published in 1972. Salk discussed ways in which science affects the larger society and explained how biological concepts can be used to examine societies as well as individuals. He defined health as being "not only . . . freedom from disease but of the wholeness of man in all the dimensions of his being." For a healthier world, he wrote, humans must make a greater effort to understand themselves and others, operating from a position of greater consciousness that promotes integrity and what Salk calls "our potential for nobility." This book continues to spark discussions about the concepts of brain/mind and has been included on reading lists for college philosophy courses.

Salk's second book, *The Survival of the Wisest,* came out in 1973. Again, Salk invited readers to set high standards in order to reach their potential. He urges individuals and communities to foster values such as cooperation and flexibility that can reduce acts of violence and exploitation. These same values, he wrote, can help to promote world peace. Salk expressed optimism that human beings possess the intellect and imagination to achieve wisdom. Reviews of the book commented that through his writing, Salk had shown himself to be not only a scientist but also a creative and visionary thinker.

Salk would write two more books, one of them with his youngest son, Jonathan, who had studied child development at Harvard University and earned a degree in anthropology from Stanford

University. Their book, *World Population and Human Values: A New Reality,* was published in 1983. It describes population patterns throughout history and discusses values that could maximize human potential while adjusting to changes in the world's population. Salk's fourth book, *Anatomy of Reality: Merging of Intuition and Reason,* was published that same year. Here Salk put into words some of his ideas about the interdependency of logic and intuition and how the two might work to produce new insights. Discussing this topic in an interview he said, "Reason alone will not serve. Intuition alone can be improved by reason but reason alone without intuition can easily lead the wrong way."

The subject of international peace appeared often in his books, and Salk's personal commitment led him to join organizations that advocate better relationships among nations and nuclear disarmament. They include International Physicians for the Prevention of Nuclear War, the Nuclear Weapons Freeze Campaign, and Physicians for Social Responsibility. While addressing civic organizations and international groups, Salk discussed ideas for alleviating hunger, poverty, disease, and war, which he called the "cancer of the world." Salk also joined the board of directors of the MacArthur Foundation, which was founded in 1978 by John D. and Catherine T. MacArthur. It ranks among the 10 largest philanthropic organizations in the United States.

In 1977 Salk attended a special ceremony at the White House. For his ongoing contributions to health and science, President Jimmy Carter awarded him the Presidential Medal of Freedom, which is the nation's highest civilian award. In presenting the medal, President Carter said, "Because of his tireless work, untold hundreds of thousands who might have been crippled are sound in body today." Salk was pleased to receive his award on the same day that the late civil rights leader, the Rev. Dr. Martin Luther King, Jr., assassinated in 1968, was honored. Salk greatly admired King as a person who made the world a better place. When he accepted his own medal, Salk praised King's efforts on behalf of what Salk called "the ultimate freedoms we seek, freedom from exploitation and oppression." He went on to say, "Without freedom from oppression and from disease, the pursuit of happiness has little meaning."

In 1977 Jonas Salk received the Presidential Medal of Freedom from President Jimmy Carter. (Corbis)

During that same speech Salk noted, "Laurels are not to be rested upon. They crown what is valued and desired by society. They impose responsibility as well as offer encouragement." He himself could look back on many laurels and several decades of achievement. There was still much to do, however, on the scientific and humanitarian fronts. The next decade would find Salk tackling a new disease.

Old and New Horizons

By the 1980s Jonas Salk was pursuing scientific areas that had interested him for years as well as heading in some new directions. Concern about the devastating effects of HIV/AIDS led him to study that syndrome. For the next six years, he worked to understand and combat the virus associated with AIDS.

"The Salk," as the institute is often called, was also moving in a new direction. It had shifted away from the idea of including scholars who specialize in the humanities and decided to focus on pure sciences. Salk researchers were making important contributions to the fields of genetics, immunology, and neurology, among other things. Neuroscience, another enduring interest of its founder, Jonas Salk, became its major focus. Along with his work and ideas, the institute would be a significant part of Salk's legacy.

Fighting AIDS

Since the 1960s Salk had focused on cancer and multiple sclerosis (MS). He hoped that new knowledge about the immune system would show scientists how to block the damaging inflammation response that occurs in MS and other autoimmune diseases. His studies on the immunological aspects of multiple sclerosis have helped other researchers who continue to seek treatments and a cure for the disease.

In 1986 Salk announced that he was studying another condition that involved the immune system, though in a different way: AIDS (acquired immune deficiency syndrome), a devastating condition that has become a public health problem around the world. Most scientists believe that a virus called HIV (for human immunodeficiency virus) causes AIDS, so the syndrome is sometimes called HIV/AIDS. HIV attacks the immune system, destroying vital cells that fight diseases. People with this condition are left with weakened immune systems. They are less able to fight off pneumonia, influenza, and other infections, as well as cancer.

According to the Centers for Disease Control (CDC), the earliest known case of HIV in a human was found in a blood sample taken in 1959 from a man who lived in the Democratic Republic of the Congo in Africa. The first cases of AIDS may have occurred in the United States during the 1970s. In 1982 U.S. public health officials began to use the term *acquired immunodeficiency syndrome,* abbreviated as AIDS, to describe the condition. Since the early 1980s the number of cases has increased each year.

AIDS is spread through contact with infected blood and in the body fluids that are carried from person to person during sexual activities. People who use intravenous (IV) drugs have contracted AIDS by injecting themselves with needles that were used by infected people. Pregnant women with AIDS can pass it on to their unborn children. AIDS also is spread in blood transfusions when people receive blood during surgery or after heavy blood loss due to accidents or hemophilia (a disease in which the blood does not clot properly when bleeding occurs). Since the mid-1980s, new tests for AIDS have been required before donated blood is approved for transfusions.

Salk, shown here working at the Salk Institute, focused on AIDS research during the 1980s. (The Salk Institute for Biological Studies)

This complex condition has been difficult to study. As scientists studied HIV, they found that it is a retrovirus. This type of virus infects cells by replacing the attacked cell's DNA genetic instructions with its own viral RNA. Such a change in the cell's instructions may take months or years to show up. When it takes effect, it causes AIDS viruses to grow in the infected cells. The viruses destroy their own cells and fool the immune system into attacking healthy cells. This virus also often mutates—changes its form. Scientists are not sure how many variations of the virus exist, and this further complicates AIDS research.

Salk intended to use his experience in virology and immunology to explore ways to prevent and/or treat AIDS. Other scientists at the Salk Institute were also pursuing various aspects of AIDS research, so there were opportunities for collaboration. Early in this endeavor, Salk considered the possibility of using killed-virus vaccines for AIDS that would contain various viral proteins. A problem arose when the process of killing the virus seemed to rip off its protein shell. Salk thought that a vaccine might require proteins from the core of the virus in order to produce an immune response. He noted that infected people who had a high level of antibodies to the proteins in the AIDS viral shell still had AIDS. Salk discussed this research when he attended the Fifth International AIDS Conference, held in Canada in 1987.

That year Salk wrote an article entitled "Prospects for the Control of AIDS by Immunizing Seropositive Individuals" for the June 1987 issue of *Nature,* a scientific journal. In the article he proposed trying a vaccine on people who were already HIV positive, because symptoms of AIDS may not occur until months or years after someone is infected. As he developed this idea further, Salk applied for a patent on an experimental vaccine and cofounded a biotechnology company called Immune Response Corporation, based in Carlsbad, California. This company planned to produce and market the vaccine, if and when it was developed.

Other researchers tried different approaches. Some worked on vaccines that do not use the whole virus. Research also has been done with subunit vaccines—genetically engineered vaccines that use copies of tiny, harmless bits of virus. Still other AIDS researchers considered making vaccines from the cowpox material that is used to vaccinate people from smallpox. Some wondered if the adenovirus that causes colds could be altered to make a harmless vaccine that would imitate the AIDS virus.

In 1989 Salk collaborated with AIDS researcher Dr. Clarence J. Gibbs, a virologist at the Neurology Institute of the National Institutes of Health. As he had done during his polio studies, Salk worked with chimpanzees, the only laboratory mammals that get AIDS. Salk and Gibbs found a killed whole-virus preparation that produced a rise in the chimps' antibodies. Then they conducted tests with 19 college students whose blood tests were HIV positive, meaning they had been exposed to the virus. These people also had poorly functioning immune systems. After a year, only one of them had developed symptoms of AIDS, and eight of them had better functioning immune systems than when the tests began. Immune Response Corporation later produced HIV immunotherapeutic, an immune-based therapy based on Salk's research. This product was not a true vaccine but rather a treatment that aimed to delay or prevent AIDS symptoms in people who were already infected.

That year AIDS reached what scientists consider epidemic levels. The World Health Organization (WHO) estimated more than 5 million cases worldwide. About 40 percent of these people were under age 25. Salk said that he was encouraged by his own research and other studies that offered hope to people with HIV.

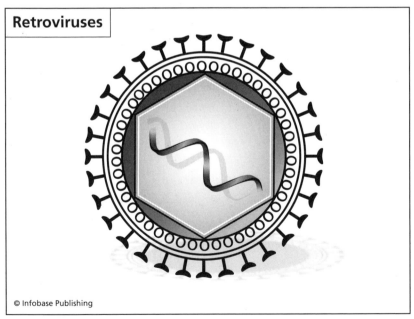

Retroviruses

© Infobase Publishing

The virus that causes AIDS belongs to the group known as retroviruses.

T Cells at Work

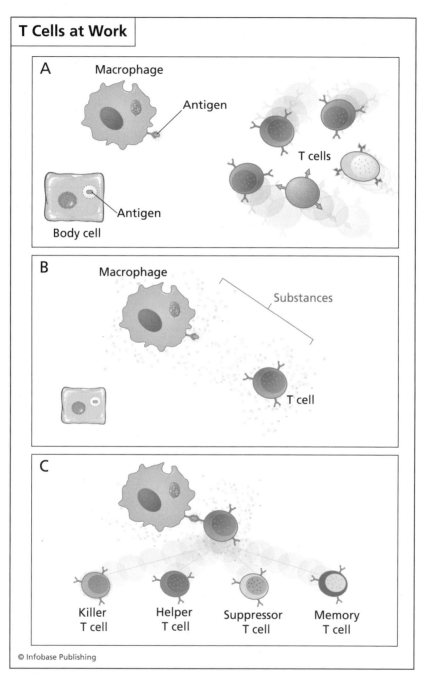

Specific Defense System: A) Antigen on an abnormal body cell, or displayed in a macro-phage, that must be recognized by T cells; B) Macrophage and T cell then secrete sub-stances that activate the T cell; C) The activated T cell duplicates itself into a subgroup.

In a 1990 interview Salk discussed the challenges still facing AIDS researchers. He noted that AIDS viruses "oppose the defense mechanism that we otherwise erect against them . . . [and] impair the immune system. Not only that, I think that it even induces the immune system to form an antibody that protects the virus." This was his rationale for seeking effective ways to vaccinate people after they were infected with HIV/AIDS rather than before. He suggested that researchers look for ways to build or enhance the body's defense mechanisms before serious damage occurs due to HIV infection.

Along those lines, Salk noted that the first reaction of the immune system after infection with the virus occurs among the T cells. It is a cell-mediated immunity called the TH1 response. As the infectious process continues, the immune system makes antibodies, leading to a humoral immunity. Referring to this process, Salk concluded, "We have to find out a way of keeping the immune system in the TH1 mode." During his own experiments with people who tested positive for the HIV virus, Salk had observed something significant when these people received inactivated HIV: Some of them had a local skin reaction—a red wheal, showing sensitivity to an antigen, that is part of a TH1 response. In these patients AIDS did not progress as quickly or severely as in those who did not have the skin reaction. Salk described these findings in meetings with other researchers and they were widely discussed.

As his work continued, Salk acknowledged another difficulty in developing vaccines: Because the parasitic AIDS virus gets inside cells, other kinds of vaccines, which work to neutralize cell-free viruses, seem unfeasible. Salk stated that a vaccine capable of halting the body's immune response in the TH1 stage would use very small doses of HIV. He optimistically predicted, "Even if that is difficult, we will find a way."

Testing AIDS vaccines also presents special challenges. Like many types of cancer, the disease may take a long time to develop in humans. That means that scientists cannot judge the effects of a vaccine as quickly as they can with influenza or polio. Scientists discussed these problems in Amsterdam at the Eighth International AIDS conference in July 1992. Salk described some tests he had conducted with research monkeys. When they received inactivated HIV vaccine meant to produce the highest levels of immunity, they still could not resist later infection with the AIDS virus. This provided researchers with more evidence that other approaches were needed.

By 1992 an estimated 10 million people around the world had HIV/AIDS, which went on to reach levels scientists call pandemic. New treatments were being used that could help to prolong the lives of people with HIV but no cure or preventive vaccine was available. Salk had hoped to see more progress during his lifetime. But with characteristic optimism, during the early 1990s Salk stated:

> *I cannot imagine that we will not be able to think the way the virus does and figure out how to outsmart the virus. . . . Solutions come . . . through asking the right question, because the answer preexists. It is the question that we have to define and discover.*

Global Health Concerns

While Salk was looking for ways to prevent or blunt the effects of HIV/AIDS and collaborating with researchers around the world, he remained active in other matters involving public health, especially immunizations. His global role in this field was reflected in his title at the University of California at San Diego, where he was appointed Distinguished Professor in International Health Sciences in 1988. Besides teaching new generations of medical students about global health concerns, Salk worked directly with international health agencies, as well as local and national groups. He advised them on ways to control infectious diseases and supported research that would provide better vaccines for children. Salk also assisted health officials with planning and carrying out immunization programs in places where polio and other infectious diseases posed a threat.

Polio had been eradicated in developed nations, but certain parts of Asia, Africa, Central and South America, and the Middle East continued to experience polio epidemics during the 1980s. The Sabin oral vaccine was being used to eliminate polio in these regions. Since oral vaccine must be refrigerated, it was difficult to transport and store. People needed to determine if it was still potent on arrival, because exposure to heat could cause problems. A special heat-sensitive device that attached to vaccine containers was developed to address this problem. Other issues arose because oral vaccine must be given in doses that are spaced out over a period of months. People who lived far from vaccination centers might not be willing or able to return. In regions with high rates of poverty and disease, people also may have numerous viruses in their bodies at any given time. Competing microorganisms can prevent live but weakened polioviruses in oral vaccine from taking hold. In these kinds of situations killed-virus (inactivated) vaccine has some advantages, and it need not be refrigerated.

The year 1979 marked the last reported wild case of polio in the Western Hemisphere. Since then the few cases that have occurred were traced to the virus contained in doses of live oral vaccine. Children who received the vaccine did not get polio, but a vulnerable adult member of the household was infected. Those who developed polio were at high risk, either because they were elderly, were taking drugs that suppressed the immune system, or had diseases that impair immunity.

Salk welcomed the arrival of a new killed-virus/inactivated polio vaccine developed by Dutch scientist A. L. Van Wezel during the 1980s. This was a stronger version of the type of vaccine that Salk developed during the 1950s and 1970s. Together with other scientists, Salk formed an organization called the Forum for the Advancement of Immunization Research. It tested the Van Wezel vaccine in Mali and what was then the Upper Volta region in the Soviet Union. Two doses of this vaccine appeared to provide full immunity.

Salk continued to question the reasoning behind the switch to Sabin's weakened-virus polio vaccine. In a 1991 interview he said:

> *It's clear now, from everything we know, that it is safer and more certain to vaccinate by injection than by mouth. . . . If you give it by injection, then you know what you are putting in. You know the effect that it is going to have, whereas if you give it by mouth, you don't know whether or not the virus is going to become activated in a pathogenic way, in the sense of causing the disease either in the recipients, or in contacts.*

In a cover article published March 29, 1954, *Time* magazine had called Jonas Salk "Polio Fighter." He was still carrying on that fight on many fronts at this point in his life.

Honors and Disappointments

Decades after Salk's polio vaccine came into use, many people still called him a hero. His name appeared on lists of "most admired people" "best-known scientists" and "most-respected Americans." He remained one of the best-known scientists in the country. In a 1968 book, *Heroes for Our Times,* members of the Overseas Press Club of America named Jonas Salk as one of the "12 heroes of our time," along with Winston Churchill, Mahatma Gandhi, Franklin D. Roosevelt, Eleanor Roosevelt, and Dr. Albert Schweitzer. The text defined heroes as "individuals who should be held up as models . . . the men and women who have left the greatest mark for good upon these times."

Salk may have hoped to receive the Nobel Prize in physiology or medicine. He was nominated but never selected. Albert Sabin also was nominated but did not win the prize. The only Nobel Prize for polio-related research was awarded to John Enders, Frederick Robbins, and Thomas Weller. Sabin often claimed that Salk did not deserve this honor. He claimed that Salk's work on the killed-virus vaccine used existing scientific techniques, and the Nobel Prize was reserved for scientific breakthroughs. Salk, Sabin stated further, had not done any new or original work. Other people said that Salk deserved the prize. According to founder Alfred Nobel, the awards should honor people who make contributions "for the good of humanity." Supporters said Salk had used creativity and courage, along with scientific know-how, to produce the polio vaccine. His work surely benefited humankind.

Salk also never was inducted into the prestigious National Academy of Sciences in the United States. This must have been disappointing, since he had developed a vaccine that saved lives and then founded and built up a world-renowned scientific institute.

Despite these slights, Salk continued to receive praise from many other colleagues, from various organizations, and from average citizens. People approached him in restaurants or on the street to thank him. During his lifetime Salk received numerous awards for his scientific work and contributions to public health. These awards include the Robert Koch medal, the Mellon Institute Award, a United States Presidential Citation, and a Congressional Gold Medal. France

In 1995 Salk attended an event at Rackham Auditorium at the University of Michigan to mark the 40th anniversary of the vaccine field trials announcement. (Bentley Historical Library, University of Michigan, Photo by Bob Kalmbach)

named him a chevalier (knight) of the Legion of Honor. Salk received honorary degrees from colleges in the United States, Britain, Israel, Italy, and the Philippines. He was inducted into the Hall of Science and Exploration of the Academy of Achievement in 1976. He received the Wright Prize for interdisciplinary study in science and engineering. This prize is awarded by Harvey Mudd College and the H. Dudley Wright Foundation based in Geneva, Switzerland. It goes to scientists and engineers who achieve excellence in interdisciplinary work or research. In 1985 President Ronald Reagan declared May 6 Dr. Jonas E. Salk Day. Reagan urged people to recognize and appreciate Salk's "tremendous contributions to society, particularly for his epochal role in the discovery of the first licensed vaccine for poliomyelitis . . . "

Salk also was honored for his humanitarian efforts. He received the Nehru Award for International Understanding and was the first person to receive the Jihan Sadat Peace Award from the Women's International Center (WIC). In 1991 Salk said that the social problem that concerned him most was "man's inhumanity to man."

In 1993 Salk returned to the city where he had developed his famous vaccine. A ceremony in the auditorium at the University of Pittsburgh marked the unveiling of Salk's portrait in the medical complex near Salk Hall. Two years later, the March of Dimes initiated a new award in Salk's honor. The March of Dimes Prize in Developmental Biology is given annually to a researcher or team whose scientific work contributes significantly to the study of birth defects. Winners receive a special medal and $250,000. In 2006 the U.S. Post Office issued a new 63-cent stamp in honor of Jonas Salk, Medical Scientist.

A Hero Remembered

After a full and extraordinary life, Jonas Salk died on June 23, 1995, of congestive heart failure. He was 80 years old.

Friends remembered the scientist and the man. They described him as kind, gentle, and concerned about humankind. Valerie Stallings, who had been a research technician at the Salk Institute for 20 years, said, "He always had an open door. . . . He was a very gracious man." Dr. Lewis Judd, head of the psychiatry department at the University of San Diego, remarked, "He was such a vital, active and alive person." Dr. Francis Crick, world-famous geneticist and one of the original institute fellows, praised Salk's lifelong efforts. He said, "Few have made one discovery that has benefited humanity so greatly. Jonas was a man who, right to his last day, was actively in pursuit of another."

A special issue of *Time* magazine dated March 29, 1999, featured Salk's picture on the cover, along with Albert Einstein and Sigmund Freud. Inside, *Time* listed him as one of the century's "100 Most Important Scientists and Thinkers." No other polio researcher was on the list. Author Wilfrid Sheed noted that Salk stood out from the crowd because of the speed with which he succeeded in developing his vaccine as well as "the honors he did not receive for doing so."

On April 12, 2005, the Smithsonian Institution rang a bell on its oldest building to signal the opening of an exhibit at the National Museum of American History about Salk and the polio vaccine. The University of Pittsburgh and the Salk Institute were among the places that held special commemorative ceremonies. Newspapers and magazines marked the occasion, and new books about Salk and polio were published throughout the year.

In a 1980 interview Jonas Salk remarked, "I don't feel like a hero, but I know that's how people feel about me." To the parents and children of the 1950s, Salk was indeed a hero. He removed the fear that they or their loved ones might be paralyzed or killed by polio. The disease could have harmed thousands more people had Salk's vaccine not become available in 1955, six years before Sabin's.

A desire to improve lives inspired Jonas Salk to pursue medical research and look for ways to fight deadly viruses. It motivated him to develop an institute that would expand that work and continue to benefit humankind. Salk urged future generations to carry on this effort:

> *My hope lies in seeing the emergence of a new generation of young people who were born into a new context with new opportunities and new circumstances. They, in my judgment, are going to act appropriately to improve the conditions of their lives and the lives of others.*

Through his own life, Jonas Salk set such an example. He worked to improve the physical and mental health of future generations so that they might also have the opportunity to develop their talents and reach their potential.

Conclusion:

Making a Difference

From their first meeting aboard the ocean liner *Queen Mary* in 1951, Basil O'Connor liked and admired Jonas Salk. O'Connor once remarked, "Jonas . . . is aware of the world and concerned about it. He sees beyond the microscope." Salk's youngest son, Jonathan, has stated that the greatest gift his father gave to his sons and to the rest of the world was his firm belief that medical research should "address problems of humankind" and "make a difference."

The Salk vaccine trial of 1954 was a unique scientific event. Never in history had so many people helped to fund medical research or volunteered to test the results of that research. Salk brought efficiency, fresh ideas, and practical knowledge to the fight against polio. He put together the relevant research and organized a team of outstanding people who used the killed-virus approach to develop a vaccine faster than other polio researchers.

Their vaccine saved thousands of people from death or paralysis and ended the terror that had plagued America for more than 40 years. Untold numbers of people around the globe also benefited from the vaccine.

The development of Salk's vaccine and the successful nationwide trials affected society in significant ways. People became more aware of science and scientific research, as well as the power of immunization. They became accustomed to the idea of preventing disease through immunization, especially during childhood. Since then effective vaccines have been developed for measles, mumps, rubella, hepatitis, and various types of influenza.

That spring day in 1955 when the vaccine was declared safe and effective was a proud one for American science and the public spirit. As a national hero, Salk inspired future generations of physicians and scientific researchers. The image of this energetic, caring doctor inspired many young people to follow careers in medicine and science.

After 1955 Salk moved on to new challenges. As a scientist, he advanced the fields of virology and immunology. He worked to prove his belief that noninfectious vaccines could protect people against viral illnesses despite the majority opinion that a live virus was necessary. Killed-virus—called inactivated—vaccines have since become more common. Today they are given to protect people against hepatitis, rabies, and other diseases. Salk encouraged a new approach to AIDS research by suggesting that a therapeutic vaccine could help to control the disease after infection occurs. Scientists are continuing to explore this idea.

Salk also is regarded as one of the founders of the scientific field called psychoneuroimmunology—the study of how the human mind, nervous system, and immune system interact. After observing similarities between the cells of the immune system and those of the central nervous system, Salk suggested that diseases involve interrelationships among the genetic system, nervous system, immune system, and behavior. He suggested further that the nervous and immune systems might follow similar patterns of development.

During his lifetime Salk compared human biology and illness to the problems that affect the larger society and harm its collective health. He once said that humans need to develop " . . . the means for prevention of those ills in the human condition that arise from active processes of disease, from active frustration of man's potential, or from its passive nonfulfillment." As an example, Salk cited people who sell illegal drugs and try to force more people to become addicts in order to increase their profits.

Today epidemiologists study not only infectious diseases such as influenza but also social problems, such as drug and alcohol abuse, that impair the health of many people. They investigate the number of people who die as a result of violence. For example, at the Centers for Disease Control (CDC) in Atlanta, epidemiologists have studied the relationship between urban violence and high murder rates among African-American teenage males in the United States.

Jonas Salk's legacy stretches far beyond the polio vaccine, his own research, and his writings, since the work of the Salk Institute for Biological Studies goes on. He aimed to help people in practical ways, and the Salk Institute carries on that work. A colleague once said, "He is the only man in the world who could have put this Institute together. . . . The scientific and social issues that interest him are important." There is no way to measure the ultimate effect the Salk Institute will have on human health and well-being. Since it was founded, the institute has trained five scientists who subsequently won Nobel Prizes. At least seven people who held positions as nonresident fellows or served on the faculty of the institute are Nobel laureates. Scientists from "the Salk" have gone on to teach and to direct other research centers, which extends its work still further.

Salk himself called the institute "a crucible of creativity." He said that in the beginning " . . . people questioned it, and said, 'Scientists work in laboratories, they look into microscopes, they work in basements.' And I said, 'Yes, that's true. I did all that myself but I want to see what happens if you do the experiment the other way.'" Salk saw the value of bringing together people from different disciplines so they can share their expertise and perspectives. Merging knowledge from different fields has become increasingly common since the mid-20th century. For example, biologists,

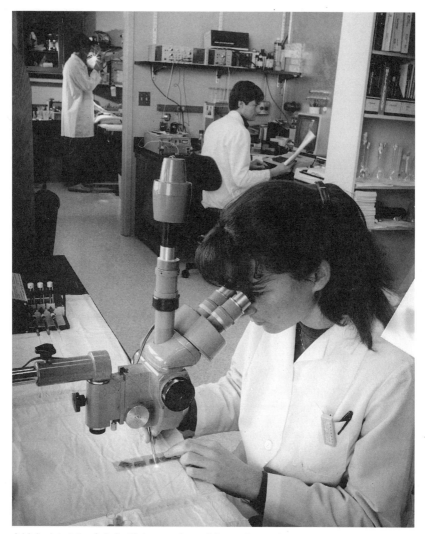

A biologist at the Salk Institute examines slides under a microscope. (The Salk Institute for Biological Studies; photo by Jim Cox)

chemists, and physicists have worked together to study living cells and molecules, such as DNA. Some key techniques used to identify and develop vaccines based on the protein composition of viruses came about through collective research.

As of 2007 the Salk Institute encompassed three research buildings with 537,000 square feet (49,889 meters^2). The institute had a

The End of Polio?

As of 1988 polio was endemic in 125 countries, with about 1,000 new cases per day. A group of organizations united with Rotary International to form the Global Campaign to End Polio. With cooperation from local and national leaders, they began mass vaccination programs. This global effort involved millions of people, mostly volunteers, who transported vaccine and immunized children. They traveled in war-torn regions and to remote places, often by canoe or bicycle, carrying cold-storage boxes of oral vaccine.

Africa was a major focus. In 1996 Nelson Mandela supported a massive plan for that continent called "Kick Polio Out of Africa." During 2001 nearly 85,000 workers in Congo set out to vaccinate 12 million children under age five.

These global efforts paid off. In 1995 China recorded no cases of polio for the first time in history. Four years later, millions of people had been vaccinated, and the number of cases of polio worldwide dropped to 20,000.

Countries still at high risk in 2002 included India, Pakistan, Somalia, Sudan, and the Democratic Republic of Congo. In Uttar Pradesh, located in India, more than 1,000 new polio cases occurred—66 percent of the worldwide total for that year. The committee organized National Immunization Days in India. Prime Minister Rajiv Gandhi called the program a living memorial to his mother, Indira Gandhi, who had been assassinated in 1984. The government worked at all levels to distribute vaccine and supplies and then provide immunizations. The dates were scheduled in advance. Volunteers in various communities publicized the dates and went door-to-door to remind people.

In 2003 about 700 cases of polio were reported, mostly in India, Pakistan, and Nigeria. The committee looked forward to reaching its goal of zero polio cases by the end of 2005, but the fight continued into 2006 as seen in the table. In September of that year, millions of children in the Horn of Africa were vaccinated during a synchronized campaign in Ethiopia, Somalia, and Kenya.

full-time faculty numbering 56, with a scientific staff of more than 850 people, including visiting scientists and students in its undergraduate, graduate, and post-doctoral programs. The major areas of research at the institute focus on three areas: molecular biology and genetics, neurosciences, and plant biology. Scientists conduct research in association with clinical centers throughout the world. Students and scientists from around the world also come to study there to improve their research skills.

The Salk Institute specializes in molecular biology and neurosciences and has been ranked as the top institution in the world in those fields. Salk researchers have expanded knowledge about cancer, birth defects, language development, genetics, viral infections, and memory loss, to name a few. Their work on autoimmune diseases, the brain, and the peripheral nervous system has received high praise. In recent years scientists have investigated the potential dangers of genetically modified (called genetically engineered) foods, examined how hormones affect metabolism, and studied the effects of different forms of exercise on the mental decline associated with aging.

CASES OF POLIO, BY COUNTRY, THE WEEK OF SEPTEMBER 27, 2006 (FROM WORLD HEALTH ORGANIZATION)

Country	Cases	Compared to same period in 2005	Date of onset of most recent case
Nigeria	836	451	August 11, 2006
India	323	30	August 29, 2006
Somalia	31	2	July 19, 2006
Afghanistan	26	4	July 24, 2006
Namibia	20	0	June 26, 2006
Pakistan	20	17	September 3, 2006
Ethiopia	14	16	July 18, 2006
Bangladesh	13	0	July 24, 2006
Niger	10	4	July 12, 2006
DRC	7	0	June 19, 2006
Indonesia	2	240	February 20, 2006
Nepal	2	0	August 1, 2006
Yemen	1	470	February 2, 2006
Angola	1	7	June 27, 2006

In 1996, the year after Salk died, the Centers for Disease Control (CDC) decided to phase out the Sabin oral vaccine and return to inactivated vaccine made with killed viruses. The U.S. Advisory Committee on Immunization Practices noted that each year about a dozen people in the United States were contracting vaccine-related polio. Though Sabin's oral vaccine had helped to end polio around the world, it was responsible for at least several new cases each year. A few cases of polio still occurred when physicians used a mixed approach with both vaccines. In 2000 the CDC advised physicians to switch to injected vaccine and use Sabin vaccine only in very special cases. Dr. Darrell Salk commented, "My father would have been pleased." In its October 13, 2004, issue, the *Journal of the American Medical Association* reported that no new cases of vaccine-related polio had occurred in the United States since 2000, when this CDC policy took effect.

Jonas Salk liked to say, "I feel that the greatest reward for success is the opportunity to do more." His ideas, work, and life continue to inspire. The scientific institute that bears his name will go on providing new tools to fight diseases and improve human lives.

CHRONOLOGY

1580–1350 B.C.E.	Archaeological evidence shows that polio existed in ancient times.
1789	Michael Underwood gives the first clinical description of polio.
1796	Edward Jenner develops the first vaccine, made for smallpox.
1887	Polio epidemic occurs in Sweden.
1908	Karl Landsteiner isolates virus that causes polio.
October 28, 1914	Jonas Salk is born in New York City.
1916	Largest U.S. epidemic to that date in New York City.
1921	Future president Franklin Delano Roosevelt survives polio and is left paralyzed.
1927	Roosevelt forms the Warm Springs Foundation to serve people with polio.
1929	Salk graduates from high school and enters City College of New York.
1934	Salk enters New York University Medical School.

1938–39   Salk works in the research laboratory of Dr. Thomas Francis at New York University.

1939   Salk receives medical degree and marries Donna Lindsay.

Warm Springs Foundation becomes the National Foundation for Infantile Paralysis (NFIP).

1939–41   Salk completes two-year internship at Mount Sinai Hospital in New York.

1941–46   Salk works with Thomas Francis at the University of Michigan to develop influenza vaccine; conducts epidemiological studies for U.S. military after World War II.

1947   Salk accepts position as director of the Virus Research Laboratory at the University of Pittsburgh.

1948   Salk receives NFIP grant and begins research for the poliovirus typing program.

1949   Drs. John Enders, Fred Robbins, and Tom Weller succeed in growing polioviruses in nonnervous tissue cultures.

1950   Salk applies for NFIP grant to fund new research for the development of a polio vaccine.

1951   Salk's Pittsburgh team completes its work typing polioviruses and develops killed-virus preparations that can prevent polio in test monkeys.

1952   Worst polio epidemic in U.S. history strikes nearly 58,000 people.

Salk tests his vaccine on people who have already had polio.

1953   Salk tests vaccine on people who never had polio.

1954   NFIP sponsors nationwide field trials of Salk's vaccine involving more than 1.8 million schoolchildren.

**April 12,
1955**   Dr. Thomas Francis announces at Ann Arbor, Michigan, that Salk's vaccine is safe and effective.

1956   Albert Sabin begins testing his live-virus oral polio vaccine in the Soviet Union.

1960   Salk leaves the University of Pittsburgh to develop a scientific institute in San Diego.

1961–62   Sabin's polio vaccine is approved for use.

1963   The Salk Institute for Biological Studies is officially founded as a nonprofit organization.

A total of 396 polio cases is reported in the United States.

1965   Salk resigns as president of Salk Institute to begin serving as director.

1968   Donna and Jonas Salk are divorced.

Salk is appointed adjunct professor in health sciences at the University of California at San Diego.

1970   Salk marries French artist Françoise Gilot.

1972   Salk's book *Man Unfolding* is published.

1973   Salk's second book, *The Survival of the Wisest,* is published.

1975   Salk's title at the institute changes to founding director.

1977   President Jimmy Carter awards Salk the Presidential Medal of Freedom.

1979	Salk joins the board of directors of the MacArthur Foundation.
1981	Salk and his son Jonathan collaborate on the book *World Population and Human Values: A New Reality.*
1983	Salk's fourth book, *Anatomy of Reality*, is published.
1985	Rotary International launches PolioPlus, a worldwide effort to immunize all children against polio.
1988	Salk announces that he is working on AIDS research.
	The World Health Organization, UNICEF, and U.S. Centers for Disease Control and Prevention, unite with Rotary International to launch the Global Polio Eradication Initiative.
1991	Scientists declare Western Hemisphere is free of polio.
June 23, 1995	Jonas Salk dies at age 80 in San Diego.
2000	Only 2,979 cases of polio are reported around the world and 550 million people have been vaccinated.
	CDC advises switching back to inactivated polio vaccine rather than the oral attenuated-virus version.
2004	Epidemiologists report that no new cases of vaccine-related polio have occurred in the United States since 2000, when the CDC stated that inactivated polio vaccine should replace oral vaccination.

GLOSSARY

adjuvant   a material or group of materials, such as chemicals or minerals, that can boost the immune-producing capacity of a vaccine

antibiotic   a substance made by fungi, bacteria, or other microbes that can decrease the growth of or kill other microbes. Amoxicillin is one example of an antibiotic used to treat bacterial diseases.

antibody   a protein manufactured by the immune system in response to the presence of foreign antigens, viruses, or bacterial toxins that binds with these substances in order to kill or neutralize them

antigen   a substance capable of activating the formation of a specific antibody against itself

attenuation   the weakening or loss of the disease causing properties of viruses and bacteria used in order to produce vaccines that will arouse an immune response without causing death or serious illness in the recipient

autopsy   examination of the body after death to determine or confirm causation

bacteria (sing: **bacterium**)   single-cell microscopic organisms that come in various shapes

chromosome   a threadlike linear body found in the nucleus of plant and animal cells that carries the genes and functions in transmitting hereditary information

culture   (v) to grow microbes in the laboratory, often using test tubes or plates that contain broth or special nutrients (for bacteria) or using tissues of living cells (for viruses)

epidemic   a widespread disease or sudden outbreak of disease that spreads to infect large numbers of people

epidemiology   the study of the causes, sources, and distributions of various diseases

electron microscope   a powerful microscope that magnifies by using a beam of electrons (negatively charged particles) rather than light rays, and magnetic fields rather than glass lenses

fermentation   a chemical reaction in which sugar is changed into carbon dioxide and alcohol by means of yeast

127

formaldehyde a strong disinfectant used for sterilizing hospital instruments and other medical and scientific purposes

formalin a solution made of formaldehyde and water; used by Salk and others to kill polioviruses in vaccine preparations

gene basic physical unit of heredity located on the chromosome that specifically influences the hereditary traits of an organism

immunity resistance to a disease-causing agent, such as a virus or bacteria, which can be natural—inborn or acquired as a result of disease—or acquired through artificial means, such as vaccination

immunology the science and medical field that deals with immunity and allergy

ingrafting the process of removing matter (in the case of vaccination, infectious material) from one site and inserting it into another in order to propagate those cells in the new site

iron lung an airtight machine that covers the body except for the head; used for artificial respiration when the lungs are not able to inhale and exhale on their own

lymphocytes white blood cells that function as part of the immune system to produce antibodies and transfer them to the site of antigens

microbe microorganisms that are invisible to the naked eye, including bacteria, fungi, and viruses, although viruses are not considered to be living organisms

mutation a change in the traits of an organism brought on by a change in its DNA (genetic material)

placebo an inactive, nonmedicinal substance, such as distilled water or a sugar pill, that is used in experiments for control groups that can then be compared to groups who receive the actual medicine or vaccine

tissue a group of living cells that contains the basic structure or function of a certain plant or animal organ

vaccination the process of using a vaccine to promote immunity to a specific disease

vaccine a material made up of weakened or killed (or inactivated) bacteria or viruses that is used to confer immunity

virology the study of viruses and viral illnesses

virus a submicroscopic particle consisting of a protein coat wrapped around genetic material, either DNA or RNA, that invades specific living cells in order to use that cell's materials to reproduce themselves hundreds of times

yellow fever A viral mosquito-borne disease found mostly in Africa and Central America.

FURTHER RESOURCES

Books

Carter, Richard. *Breakthrough: The Saga of Jonas Salk.* New York: Trident, 1966.

> *Detailed biography of Salk, detailing his polio research, based on extensive research and personal interviews.*

Dennis, Mark, and Christine McNab, et al. photographs by Sebastiao Salgado. *The End of Polio: A Global Effort to End a Disease.* Boston: Bulfinch Press, 2001.

> *Describes the multinational effort, which began in 1988, to eradicate polio around the world by the year 2005. Contains many first-hand accounts of polio in various countries and photographs.*

Dowling, Harry F. *Fighting Infection: Conquests of the Twentieth Century.* Cambridge, Mass.: Harvard University Press, 1977.

> *History of the diagnosis, prevention and treatment of infectious diseases during the 1900s, with information about viral diseases and the development of polio vaccines.*

Ducas, Dorothy. "Dr. Jonas Salk" in *Heroes for Our Times.* The Overseas Press Club of America (eds.) Harrisburg, Pa.: Stackpole, 1968.

> *A brief biography written by a journalist who knew Salk through her work for the National Foundation for Infantile Paralysis.*

Edelson, Edward. *The Immune System.* New York: Chelsea House, 1989.

> *For young readers. An introduction to the human immune system and the processes of natural and artificial immunity.*

Farrell, Jeanette. *Invisible Enemies: Stories of Infectious Disease.* New York: Farrar, Straus, and Giroux, 2005.

> *Historical look at seven infectious diseases and the efforts to eradicate them.*

Farrow, Mia. *What Falls Away.* New York: Knopf, 1997.

> *In her autobiography actress Mia Farrow discusses her recovery from polio at age nine and its effect on her life.*

Fishbein, Morris, et al. *A Tribute to Basil O'Connor for His 75th Birthday. March of Dimes, 1966.*

> *Contains speeches, including one by Jonas Salk, made during a special celebration in O'Connor's honor held by the March of Dimes.*

Gallagher, Hugh Gregory. *Black Bird, Fly Away: Disabled in an Able-Bodied World.* Arlington, Va.: Vandamere Press, 1994.

> *Author and political activist Gallagher describes his life after surviving paralytic polio during his teens.*

———. *FDR's Splendid Deception: The Moving Story of Roosevelt's Massive Disability—and the Intense Effort to Conceal It from the Public.* 3rd ed. Arlington, Va.: Vandemere Press, 1999.

> *A polio survivor and advocate for the disabled describes Franklin Roosevelt's battle with polio and his phenomenally successful political career despite paralysis.*

Giblin, James Cross. *When Plague Strikes: The Black Death, Smallpox, AIDS.* New York: HarperCollins, 1995.

> *For young readers, a history of three major diseases that have struck millions of people around the world.*

Gould, Tony. *A Summer Plague: Polio and Its Survivors.* New Haven, Conn.: Yale University Press, 1995.

> *Describes the decades of polio epidemics in America, the human toll, and the efforts to find a vaccine.*

Klein, Aaron E. *Trial by Fury: The Polio Vaccine Controversy.* New York: Charles Scribner's Sons, 1972.

> *Discusses the debate over the safety and effectiveness of inactivated vaccine developed by Salk versus Sabin's oral, attenuated-virus vaccine.*

Kluger, Jeffrey. *Splendid Solution: Jonas Salk and the Conquest of Polio.* New York: G. P. Putnam, 2004.

> *Biography of Jonas Salk, along with the story of the polio vaccine and vaccine trials of 1954.*

Lauren, Sompayrac. *How the Immune System Works*. 2nd ed. Oxford: Blackwell, 2003.

> *A readable discussion of basic immunology; helps to clarify complex concepts.*

McKenna, Maryn. *Beating Back the Devil: On the Front Lines with the Disease Detectives of the Epidemic Intelligence Service*. New York: Free Press, 2004.

> *Discusses the investigation of the Cutter vaccine incident of 1955.*

Meier, P. "The Biggest Public Health Experiment Ever." In J. M. Tanur, ed. *Statistics: A Guide to the Unknown*. San Francisco: Holden-Day, 1972, 2–13.

> *Discusses the polio vaccine trials.*

Offit, Paul A., M.D. *The Cutter Incident: How America's First Polio Vaccine Led to the Growing Vaccine Crisis*. New Haven, Conn.: Yale University Press, 2005.

> *Discusses the faulty vaccine that caused hundreds of cases of polio shortly after the mass immunization program was launched in 1955 and its effect on vaccine research and development.*

Oshinsky, David M. *Polio: An American Story*. New York: Oxford University Press, 2005.

> *Examines the major scientists and the role of the NFIP in the race to develop the first polio vaccine following decades of polio epidemics.*

Paul, John R. *A History of Poliomyelitis*. New Haven, Conn.: Yale University Press, 1971.

> *Comprehensive, scholarly discussion of polio through history, including the clinical aspects of the disease. Describes virus research and other findings that led to development of polio vaccines.*

Paul, William E. *Immunology: Recognition and Response, Readings from Scientific American Magazine*. New York: W. H. Freeman, 1990.

> *Prominent scientists present advanced and technical material about the immune system.*

Persico, Joseph E. *Edward R. Murrow: An American Original*. New York: Dell, 1988.

Includes description of Salk's televised interviews on Murrow's program See It Now.

Rose, David W. *The March of Dimes* (Images of America series). New York: Arcadia, 2003.

History of this successful voluntary health organization by a March of Dimes archivist.

Rowland, John. *The Polio Man: The Story of Doctor Salk.* New York: Roy Publishers, 1960.

Written for young readers; a biography that covers Salk's early years, research on viruses and polio, and development of the polio vaccine.

Salk, Jonas. *Anatomy of Reality: Merging of Intuition and Reason.* New York: Columbia University Press, 1983.

Discusses what people can do to build a promising world for future generations. Discusses how, throughout history, good has overcome evil as part of the error-correcting mechanism that permits human survival.

———. *Man Unfolding.* New York: Harper and Row, 1972.

Applying biological concepts to examine humans as individuals and as part of larger societies, Salk describes how creativity contributes to human health and the growth of healthy societies.

———. *The Survival of the Wisest.* New York, Harper and Row, 1973.

Examines how human imagination, foresight, and wisdom lead to increased self-awareness and self-discipline that can improve the quality of life.

———. *World Population and Human Values: A New Reality* (with Jonathan D. Salk). New York: Harper and Row, 1981.

Uses graphs and text to examine patterns of world population throughout history. Discusses how people's attitudes, values, and choices affect and are affected by population factors.

Sass, Edmund J., ed. *Polio's Legacy: An Oral History.* Lantham, Md.: University Press of America, 1996.

Thirty-five people describe their experiences with polio, starting with the time they were diagnosed.

Seavey, Nina Gilden, Jane S. Smith, and Paul Wagner. *A Paralyzing Fear: The Triumph Over Polio in America.* New York: TV Books, 1998.

A dramatic look at polio through interviews with people who survived the disease, worked with polio patients, or were involved in polio research.

Shorter, Edward. *The Health Century.* New York: Doubleday, 1987.

Accounts of the great medical advances that have taken place during the 20th century; includes discussion of polio vaccines and new developments in treating autoimmune diseases, cancer, and AIDS.

Smith, Jane S. *Patenting the Sun: Polio and the Salk Vaccine.* New York: William Morrow, 1990.

Combines history of polio and vaccines with biographical material about Salk. The author, a former polio pioneer, had access to Salk's personal papers and historical documents relating to the vaccine trials of 1954.

The Salk Institute for Biological Studies: Profile of a Unique Research Center: Faculty Brochure. La Jolla, Calif.: The Salk Institute. (n.d.).

Stoller, Ezra (photographer), et al. *The Salk Institute.* Princeton, N.J.: Princeton University Press, 2000.

Photographic essay; part of a series on landmarks of 20th century architecture.

Tucher, Andie, ed. *Bill Moyers, A World of Ideas, II.* New York: Doubleday, 1990.

Interview with Jonas Salk made as part of Moyers's series for public television.

Williams, Greer. *Virus Hunters.* New York: Knopf, 1959.

Engrossing history of virology and major researchers through history; includes chapter on Salk and the polio vaccine.

Internet Resources

Baum, Joan. "Celebrating the 50th Anniversary of the Salk Vaccine With Jonathan Salk." Education Update Online, May 2005. Available online. URL: http://www.educationupdate.com/archives/2005/May/html/ColFeat-Salk.html. Accessed on July 28, 2005.

Salk's son Jonathan discusses his father's scientific work.

Foege, Dr. William. "Speech on the Fiftieth Anniversary of the Polio Vaccine, upon receiving the 2005 Thomas Francis, Jr. Medal in Global

Public Health." April 12, 2005. Available online. URL: http://www.polio. umich.edu/program/foege.html. Accessed on September 21, 2006.

Describes the historic polio vaccine field trials of 1954, especially the work of Dr. Thomas Francis, Jr., and the team at the University of Michigan.

Global Polio Eradication Initiative. "The History." Available online. URL: http://www.polioeradication.org/history.asp. Accessed on March 4, 2005.

Describes the history of polio epidemics and efforts to combat the disease, including the global initiative organized by world health organizations, civic groups, government officials, and volunteers to eradicate polio by the year 2005.

"Immunization, Vaccines, and Biologicals." (World Health Organization) Available online. URL: http://www.who.int/vaccines-diseases/history/ history.shtml. Accessed on July 2, 2005.

Information about the organization's efforts to provide immunizations against infectious diseases to people around the world.

"Iron Lung Survivors." Available online. URL: http://www.geocities. com/arojann.geo/ironlung.html. Accessed on November 12, 2004.

Personal accounts by polio survivors who have remained dependent on respirators after surviving paralyzing attacks of the disease.

"Interview with Jonas Salk, M.D." Academy of Achievement. May 16, 1991. Available online. URL: http://www.achievement.org/autodoc/ page/sal0int-1. Accessed on April 4, 2005.

In this long interview, Salk discusses his life and scientific and humanitarian work, including work on the polio vaccine and The Salk Institute.

Polio Survivors Association. Available online. URL: http://www. polioassociation.org/. Accessed on June 11, 2005.

Resources for polio survivors, including information, support and shared experiences.

Takaro, Timothy. "The Man in the Middle [Basil O'Connor]." *Dartmouth Medicine Magazine*, 29, no. 1 (Fall 2004). Available online. URL: http://dartmed.dartmouth.edu/fall04/html/man_in_the_middle.shtml. Accessed on January 17, 2007.

Profile of the dynamic head of the National Foundation for Infantile Paralysis (NFIP).

University of Michigan. "Do You Remember? 50th Anniversary of the Polio Vaccine." April 2005. Available online. URL: http://www.polio.umich.edu/history/memories.html. Accessed on August 20, 2005.

Polio pioneers reflect on their experiences.

Women's International Center (WIC). "Dr. Jonas Salk." Available online. URL: http://www.wic.org/bio/jsalk.htm. Accessed on February 17, 2005.

Brief biography and material relating to the Jihan Sadat Peace Prize awarded by the WIC to Jonas Salk.

Periodicals

Blume, Stuart, and Ingrid Geesink. "A Brief History of Polio Vaccines," *Science,* June 2, 2000, pp. 1,593–1,594.

Describes the research conducted during the 1900s to produce the killed-virus and live-virus vaccines.

Collins, Huntly. "Iron Lungs and Isolation: Tales of the Polio Years." *Philadelphia Inquirer,* February 23, 1999.

A look at the effect of polio on specific patients and hospitals in the years before Salk's vaccine became available.

Elmer-Dewitt, Philip. "Reliving Polio." *Time,* March 28, 1994, pp. 54–55.

A discussion of post-polio syndrome.

Goldberg, Joan Rachel. "The Creative Mind: Jonas Salk." *Science Digest.* June 1985, pp. 51, 95.

Salk describes the experiences and insights that led him to challenge existing ideas about vaccines.

Jaret, Peter. "The Disease Detectives: Stalking the World's Epidemics." *National Geographic.* January 1991, pp. 114–140.

Dramatic stories of epidemics and public health threats around the world; the methods used to track down the sources and analyze how diseases are spread.

Johnson, George. "Once Again, A Man With a Mission." *New York Times Sunday Magazine.* November 25, 1990, pp. 57–61.

Summarizes Salk's scientific achievements, including the development of the Salk Institute; discusses his AIDS research.

"Jonas Salk Remembered as Gracious Hero of the Century." *San Diego Daily,* June 26, 1995. Available online. URL http://www.eischools.com/~llopez/salkreprint.html.

Friends and colleagues remember Salk in this article written shortly after his death.

Lott, Jeffrey. "Editor's Note," *Swarthmore Alumni Bulletin,* June 1997. Available online. URL www.swarthmore.edu/bulletin/archive/97/june97/editor.html.
Polio pioneer Jeffrey Lott describes his experiences with the Salk vaccine trials.

Lugo, Mark-Elliot. "Rebirth of the Salk Institute." *San Diego Magazine.* August 1989, pp. 104–110; 234.
History of the institute, its scientific contributions, and the plans to expand buildings and research facilities.

Paulson, Tom. "At the Salk Family Table, A Long Conquest Is Begun," *Seattle Post-Intelligencer,* April 26, 2004. Available online. URL http://seattlepi.nwsource.com/national/170630_salkson26.html.
Interviews with Salk's sons provide a first-hand view of Salk's work on the vaccine and his decision to immunize his own family.

"A Quiet Young Man's Magnificent Victory," *Newsweek,* April 25, 1955, pp. 64–67.
A contemporary account that describes Salk's role in developing the polio vaccine and the public reaction to the Ann Arbor announcement; biographical information about Salk and the history of polio research.

Sabin, Albert. "Oral Polio Vaccine: History of Its Development and Prospects for Eradication of Poliomyelitis." *Journal of the American Medical Association.* November 22, 1965, p. 853.
Sabin discusses the development of his attenuated-virus vaccine and its use around the world.

Selvaggio, Marc. "The Making of Jonas Salk." *Pittsburgh.* June 1984, pp. 43–51.
Shows how Salk and his research team developed the vaccine; describes polio outbreaks and polio research through the years; shows how the media covered events during the trials and announcements; discusses ongoing debate over live versus killed virus vaccines.

Societies and Organizations

The March of Dimes
http://www.marchofdimes.com/aboutus/aboutus.asp
1275 Mamaroneck Avenue,
White Plains, NY 10605
Telephone: (888) 663-4637

The Salk Institute for Biological Studies
http://www.salk.edu/
P.O. Box 85800
San Diego, CA 92186-5800
Telephone: (858) 453-4100

INDEX

Mali 109
Mandela, Nelson 119
Man Unfolding (Salk) 98
March of Dimes 67, 89,
90, 112
March of Dimes Prize
in Developmental
Biology 112
mass immunizations
80–86
Mayer, Adolf 26
McEllroy, William 38
Medin, Karl Oscar 5
MEF-1 strain 48
Meister, Joseph 21
memory T cell *106*
mice 42
microorganisms 18–19
microscopes 18
mineral oil adjuvant
63, 68
minorities 85–86
Mixture 199 53–54
monkey kidney, as cul-
ture 47, 53–55
monkeys, experimental
use of 36, 37, 41, 48,
107–108
Monod, Jacques 95
Montagu, Mary Wortley
17
Monteggia, Giovanni
Battista 4
Mother's March on
Polio 35
Mountain, Isabel
Morgan 50
Mount Sinai Hospital
(New York) 23
multiple sclerosis (MS)
102
Municipal Hospital,
Pittsburgh,
Pennsylvania 38, 40,
43, 62
Murrow, Edward R. 80
muscle, as poliovirus
growth culture 42
mutation 103–104

N

Nathanson, Neal 81
National Academy of
Sciences 110
National Foundation
for Infantile Paralysis
(NFIP)
early publicity on
polio vaccine 67,
68
evolution into March
of Dimes 89
field trials 65, 68–
69, 71–72
fundraising during
1952 epidemic 62
iron lungs 54
killed-virus experi-
ments 56–57
mass immunizations
80
Salk's request for
further funding
44, 47
shortfall in vaccina-
tion rate 84
testing on children
60
training for field tes-
ters 71–72
typing project 38–
40, 46
vaccine plans 47
vaccine test results
77
virus study 42
Warm Springs
Foundation and
35
Nature 104
Nehru Award for
International
Understanding 111
nerve damage 15
nervous system/im-
mune system interac-
tions 116
Netherlands 94
neutralization *13*

New Deal 37
Newsweek magazine
79
New York City 1–2, 6,
8–10
New York Health
Department 36
New York Times, The
81
*New York Times
Magazine, The* 68
New York University
Medical School
12–14
NFIP. *See* National
Foundation for
Infantile Paralysis
Nigeria 119
Nix, Robert 60, 61
Nobel, Alfred 110
Nobel Prize 43, 110,
117
nonparalytic polio 16
nucleic acid 27

O

O'Connor, Basil *34,*
34–35
daughter's polio at-
tack 43
and decline in polio
cases 93–94
early publicity on
polio vaccine 67
field trial announce-
ment 69
polio vaccine test
results 77
request for further
research from Salk
46
Salk Institute fund-
raising 90
on Salk's character
115
U.S. Medal of Merit
80
virulent vaccine inci-
dent 81–83

oil-based vaccine 68
oral vaccine. *See* Sabin
vaccine
Orgel, Leslie E. 95
orthomyxovirus *31*

P

Pakistan 119
palsy 4
pandemic 16, 108
paralysis 15
Park, William 36
Park-Brodie vaccine
36–37, 47
passive immunity 49
Pasteur, Louis 18–21,
20, 30
pasteurization 19
Paul, John R. 16
peace, international 99
Phipps, James *17*, 18
Pittsburgh,
Pennsylvania 43, 69.
See also University of
Pittsburgh
Pittsburgh Virus
Research Laboratory
40, 60–61, 78
placebo 69, 72
Poland 86
polio
cases, worldwide
(2006) 120
decline after intro-
duction of vaccine
84–86
early treatments 6,
15
history prior to 1916
2–6, *3*
identification of vi-
rus 29–30
medical debates in
early 20th century
13–16
new cases caused by
oral vaccine 121
in vaccinated chil-
dren 80–83

worldwide eradica-
tion of 108–109,
119
polio epidemics. *See*
epidemics
poliomyelitis xiii–xiv, 4
Polio Pioneers 70–73
polio research 33–44
polio survivors 57, 60,
89
polio vaccine xiii–xiv,
115–116. *See also*
killed-virus vaccine
animal testing *53*,
53–56
defective (virulent)
36–38, 75, 80–84,
94
early failures 36–38
effect on polio rate
84–86
effect on society
116
enhanced version
98
field trials 32, 68–
73, *73*, 75–79
first general use after
trials 80–84
human testing
59–73
human testing de-
bates 56–57
killed-virus v. live-
virus debate xiv,
14, 49–52, 65, 93,
94, 109
public hopes for vac-
cine 66–68
Sabin vaccine 65,
92–94, 108–109,
121
Van Wezel vaccine
109
poliovirus *5*
classification of
38–44
Simon Flexner's
work 6

growth for use in
vaccines 47–48
identification of
29–30
multiple types of
38–39
search for suitable
culture tissue
41–44
testing for dead vi-
ruses in vaccine
56–57
Polk, Pennsylvania
61–62
Post Office, U.S. 112
post-polio syndrome 89
Presidential Medal of
Freedom 99–100, *100*
production, of vaccine
70, 80–84
"Prospects for the
Control of AIDS
by Immunizing
Seropositive
Individuals" (Salk)
104
psychoneuroimmunol-
ogy 116
Public Health Service,
U.S. 82
Pugleasa, Charlene 8–9

R

rabies 21
Reagan, Ronald 111
reason, intuition and
99
respirator. *See* iron lung
retrovirus 103, *105*
Rivers, Thomas 57,
65, 77
RNA (ribonucleic acid)
27, 103
Robbins, Fred 42, 43
Roosevelt, Franklin D.
34, 34–37, *36*
Rotary International
119
Russia. *See* Soviet Union